SCOTTISH
KEERIOSITIES

ROBERT
HENDERSON

with a foreword by
JOHN RUNDLE

SAINT ANDREW PRESS
1995

Published by
SAINT ANDREW PRESS
121 George Street, Edinburgh EH2 4YN

Copyright © Robert Henderson 1995

ISBN 0 7152 0708 3

British Library Cataloguing in Publication Data
> A catalogue record for this book
> is available from the British Library

ISBN 0715207083

Design concept by Mark Blackadder.
Illustration on page 107 by Michael Turnbull.
Etchings are taken from J Grant: *Old and New Edinburgh*
(Cassell, 1887) in 3 vols; Samuel Green: *Scottish Pictures*
(Religious Tract Society, 1891); J A Wylie: *The Scots
Worthies* (Wm Mackenzie, 1880); Laurence Hutton:
Literary Landmarks of Edinburgh (Osgood & McIlvaine,
1891); 'The Scottish Annals' from Macfarlane/Thomson:
The Comprehensive History of England (Blackie & Sons
1861) in 12 vols.
Cover photographs by Robert Henderson.
Typeset in 11.5/14 pt Garamond.
Printed by Bell and Bain Ltd., Glasgow

CONTENTS

FOREWORD
by John Rundle

Occasionally people are foolish enough to say to me, 'Do you never run out of material about Scotland – it's such a small country, after all.' Small – yes, undoubtedly – but also infinitely varied: and if you don't believe that, you need only read the diverse collection of keeriosities Robert Henderson has assembled here.

The face of Scotland can change in a few miles of travel, and, in these miles, different communities have lived for a thousand or more years. That's another reason why there's so much to fascinate in Scotland – we've been around a long time doing whimsical things like building English-style holiday resorts on the Solway at the turn of the century; painting a Crucifixion scene in a cave at Campbeltown; leaving an unloved wife to drown on a rocky islet in Argyll (yes, we know how to have fun).

Prophecies, sieges, marriage customs, Europe's largest Buddhist temple – Scotland has them all, with the distinctive touch of Scottishness that intrigues folk the world over.

Those who think they know Scotland will be constantly surprised by this collection, and those who don't know Scotland will wonder why they chose to remain so ignorant of such an infinitely-absorbing nation.

Run out of material? – that certainly *would* be a curiosity!

[JOHN RUNDLE, Former Editor, *The Scots Magazine*]

PREFACE
by Robert Henderson

During the course of writing this book, I have been helped by various people in a number of different ways and I would like to offer them all my sincere thanks. The following people contributed by drawing my attention to 'keeriosities' in particular areas:

Frances and Sandy Bryce (Renfrewshire); Neil Clement (Fife and Sutherland); Betty Gibson (Lanarkshire); Jim and Annette Hunter (Selkirk and Roxburghshire); Michael Lowndes (various locations); and John Randall (Peebleshire). Dr Henry Hutchison, minister of Carmunnock Parish Church, kindly spared the time to show me the unique Orders of the Watch in the watchhouse.

Valuable and constructive comments on early drafts of the text were provided by my mother, Mary Henderson, by my late father-in-law, James Edgar, and by Harold Kyte. Sir John and Lady Clerk not only allowed me access to see the replica of Arthur's O'on, but also kindly made papers available to me at Penicuik House. I am grateful to Derek Braid for his invaluable help in a number of areas, and also to the late John Rundle, who kindly agreed to contribute a Foreword before his untimely death earlier this year.

Particular thanks are due to my sister-in-law, Anne Stiedl, who spent a considerable amount of time and effort reading each chapter and suggesting numerous improvements.

Lastly, and most important, this book could never have been completed without the tremendous support, encouragement and practical assistance of my wife, Eileen, and the tolerance of my long-suffering children, Laura and Niall. To them I owe a special debt.

FINGAL'S CAVE, FROM THE INTERIOR

INTRODUCTION

In the course of travelling around Scotland, I have come to realise that many places not on the conventional tourist circuit contain features which, though not widely known, are nevertheless well worth visiting because in some way they are unusual. Their special appeal may lie in their rarity value or, more likely, in the odd characters or unexpected stories associated with them. The items themselves may be peculiar in some way or they may mark the scene of some extraordinary event. This makes them worthy of the term 'keeriosity'. This is the Scots equivalent of the English word 'curiosity' and is defined by the dictionary as something that is 'strange or fascinating'.

I like to think that this book will contribute to a better understanding of Scotland's local historical and cultural heritage. By drawing attention to lesser known aspects of Scotland's man-made environment, I hope that both Scottish residents and visitors will be encouraged to seek out and visit those features which otherwise would be overlooked. It is perhaps surprising to discover the number of places which are associated with strange or humorous events or with eccentric individuals. All add colour to any area.

The choice of keeriosities for inclusion in

the book has been a most enjoyable but not always easy task. The qualifying factor for consideration has been that there must be something on the ground in Scotland that is visible and has an unusual or remarkable story associated with it. The stories are thought to be true, even if there is no original written verification. No doubt older tales can alter in the telling and although variants may exist, the basic ingredients remain the same. They cover such diverse subjects as caves and Cailleachs, effigies and epitaphs, the hunted and the haunted, romance and repentance, traumas and tragedies.

There are too many objects of interest to incorporate them all and new ones are continually coming to my attention. Inevitably the decision whether to include features in the book has been a personal one, depending on what has most appealed to me at the time. The omission of examples which others consider to be either of greater interest or to have more entertaining stories may well mean that I am unaware of them. Consequently I am always delighted to hear of new items.

The locations of all the keeriosities mentioned are shown in capital letters in the text. More detailed directions for finding the item referred to are shown in the Geographical Index at the back of the book. An attempt has been made to exclude those keeriosities on private properties which are not regularly open to the public. This has been done both to make it easier for visitors to see the objects mentioned, and to protect the privacy of property owners and their tenants. Inevitably perhaps there are a few exceptions and these are marked in the Directory by an asterisk. In these cases prior arrangements need to be made if the subject of interest is to be viewed.

As far as possible I have tried to verify that everything featured in the book can still be seen, but this cannot of course be guaranteed. We live in an ever-changing world and neither age, quality nor rarity value guarantees the survival and protection of our rich assortment of oddities. They can all too easily disappear. Threats to their future come from various sources. Vandalism can deface and destroy items of interest (witness the treatment meted out to the statue of the Black Dwarf in the Manor Valley). Theft is an ever present threat and accounts for the disappearance of the five distinctive stones from the grave of Shaw Mor in the graveyard at Doune, near Aviemore. Sadly, an increasing number of churches are now kept locked because of the risks of theft and vandalism. Building construction can all too easily destroy structures of particular historic significance as shown by the demolition of the unique Arthur's O'on near Stenhousemuir. Neglect also leads to the loss of unusual features as paintwork peels and old notices and signs become illegible. Natural processes of erosion and weathering are also at work, steadily obliterating many fascinating inscriptions on old gravestones.

Fortunately, all is not lost. There are many encouraging signs that give hope for the future protection and conservation of our heritage of remarkable and often eccentric items. Historic sites and buildings are now better protected from deliberate destruction or are being found new uses. Old signs are being preserved, as can be seen at Newtonmore where the notice in Gaelic commemorating a notable legal victory for the local people has recently been restored. The wording on gravestones is being recorded for posterity by enthusiastic volunteers, and in some instances 'Old Mortality's' example of recutting notable old gravestones has been followed. Interest in local history is increasing and membership of conservation and heritage organisations is growing rapidly.

Such trends augur well for the continued survival of our Scottish keeriosities.

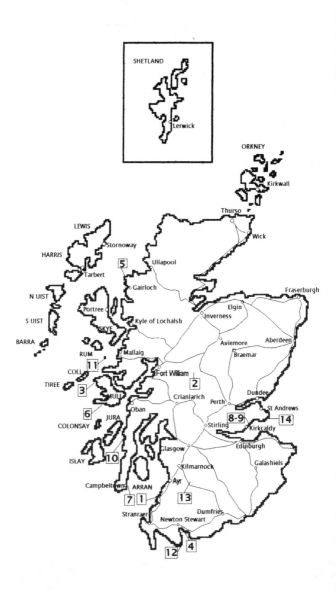

MAP 1 — CAVE-DWELLERS

CAVE-DWELLERS

Ref	Location	Description
1	Ballantrae	Sawney Bean's Cave
2	Ben Alder	Cave (Cluny's Cage) used by Bonnie Prince Charlie
3	Carsaig (Mull)	Nun's Cave
4	Carsluith	Dirk Hatteraick's Cave
5	Cove	Cave used for modern worship
6	Crakaig (Mull)	Cave with remains of illicit still
7	Davaar Island	Painting of Crucifixion in cave
8	East Wemyss	Doo Cave
9	East Wemyss	Pictish and Viking pictures in caves
10	Ellary	St Columba's Cave
11	Isle of Eigg	Cave where inhabitants of Eigg were suffocated
12	Isle of Whithorn	St Ninian's Cave
13	Lugar	Cave used for coal gas experiments
14	Pittenweem	St Fillan's Cave

CAVE-DWELLERS

Caves are usually dark, dank and distant from major centres of population. This makes them either unknown or unattractive to most people. It is precisely these same characteristics that appeal to a small group of individuals who seek solace in solitude, away from unwanted attention. Since caves appeal to individualists – and individualists are, almost by definition, regarded by every-one else as being somewhat eccentric – it is hardly surprising that caves have more than their share of strange stories. Motives for seeking refuge in caves have ranged from the noble to the nefarious.

RELIGIOUS RETREATS

The early Christian missionaries took to caves like ducks to water. They were venturing into uncharted territory where no Christian man had gone before. Caves offered shelter and privacy in a potentially unfriendly environment, and provided a base from which the missionaries could establish contact with the local community. The praying eyes of the missionaries would be undisturbed by the prying eyes of suspicious locals.

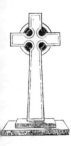

The two best known of those early men of God were St Columba and St Ninian.

Both are associated with caves. St Columba's Cave is on the shores of Loch Caolisport, to the east of **ELLARY**, Argyll & Bute, and contains a stone-built altar with a cross carved above it on the sloping roof. Scooped out of the rock floor is a hollow basin, possibly used for holding the Holy Water during Mass. It is a simple but powerful reminder of the courage and persistence of those who first brought Christianity to Scotland. Columba, who came to Scotland in the sixth century, is forever associated with the island of Iona where he was to settle and establish his monastery, which was later to become a place of pilgrimage.

Many of the stones in Iona Cathedral were carved in the Nuns' Cave, near **CARSAIG** on the neighbouring island of Mull. The stones came from the horizontal bed of sea-washed sandstone rock which is just below the cave. On the cave wall are carved religious symbols such as crosses. The cave received its name from the nuns who sheltered within it when they were expelled from Iona after the Reformation.

Whereas St Columba is associated with the Highlands in general and Iona in particular, St Ninian's connections were with Galloway, where he arrived in about AD 400. His cave, on the shore near the **ISLE OF WHITHORN**, Wigtown, also has on its walls some incised crosses, the earliest of which date from the eighth century. The cave became a place of pilgrimage and the crosses were probably religious graffiti cut by pilgrims to record their visit.

Early religious activity was not, however, confined to the west. The east of Scotland also has a cave associated with its local saint, Fillan, who was an eighth century Christian missionary. Within the cave at **PITTENWEEM**, North East Fife, is an altar and spring of, water. This shrine ceased to be used after the Reformation, but it was restored and rededicated in 1935. Services are still held periodically in the cave.

A cave that was regularly used for church services within the past century can be seen on the shores of Loch Ewe at **COVE**, Ross & Cromarty. It contained wooden seats and a pulpit and was used by local people following the 1843 Disruption when the Free Church split from the Church of Scotland.

Caves provided not only shelter and water but sometimes food as well. In mediaeval times Doo Cave at **EAST WEMYSS**, Kirkcaldy, housed pigeons to maintain a ready supply of fresh meat. The nesting boxes carved into the solid rock are still clearly visible. This cave was so renowned for the quality of its food that it merited inclusion in the local *Egon Ronay* guide of its time. This was done by including the cave in the dowry that came with the laird's daughter. The quality was due to the presence in the cave of a herb called Alexander, which appealed to the pigeon palate. It seems that this herb was used to combat scurvy so that tasty meat and a scurvy antidote was a dual benefit of these doos.

CAVES *in* ARTS *and* SCIENCE

The caves used by the early missionaries
display examples of religious artwork in the
form of carvings such as crosses, tridents
and fish, but some spectacular and curious
instances of secular artwork can also be seen
on cave walls.

There is a unique and remarkable picture
gallery on the walls of Court and Jonathan's
Caves at EAST WEMYSS, Kirkcaldy. Most of
the pictures date from Pictish times between
AD 500-900 and include crude drawings of
birds, animals, fish, sceptres and double disk
patterns – subjects which further north are
beautifully portrayed on carved Pictish stones
and slabs. There are also some fascinating
ninth century pictures attributable to the
Vikings. These include a Viking Picasso's
stylised rendering of the Norse god Thor
with his hammer and sacred goat, as well as
the oldest drawing of a boat in Britain. The
boat looks like a Viking longship, but could
just possibly be much older, dating from the
Bronze Age. Mystery is never far away from
these ancient creations by unknown artists.

A more recent mystery arose over a
painting of the Crucifixion which, in 1887,
was discovered on the rock wall of a cave on
DAVAAR ISLAND in Campbeltown Loch,
Argyll & Bute. After much local excitement
and some wild speculation as to the origins
of the picture, it transpired that the solution
to its sudden appearance lay not in the super-
natural but in the superb *natural* talent of
local artist Archibald Mackinnon. In 1934,

at the age of eighty, he returned to the cave to retouch his painting. Since then this process has been repeated by a local artist. As a result this strangely located but impressive painting is still clearly visible.

Caves have proved invaluable not only to the development of the arts, but also to science. As well as functioning as art galleries, caves have been pressed into service as scientific laboratories where work could be pursued out of the sight of suspicious laypeople or technical rivals. In the eighteenth century, a cave on the banks of the Lugar Water near LUGAR, Cumnock & Doon Valley, was used by William Murdoch as a laboratory to carry out experiments which led to the successful production of gas lighting from coal gas.

CRIMINAL CONNECTIONS

High taxes and customs dues have, through-out the ages, provided people with an incentive to avoid payment. Smuggling was a popular local pastime, particularly in coastal communities with access to cheaper imported goods. Somewhere was needed to store the contraband until it could be distributed to the markets, and where better to hide things than in a dark cave? Dirk Hatteraick's Cave, just above the sea shore near CARSLUITH, Wigtown, was one such hiding place. Inside there are elaborate stone box-like structures for storing bottles of brandy and other smuggled goods.

This cave is named after the fictional

Dirk Hatteraick, who appears in Sir Walter Scott's novel *Guy Mannering*. Scott, however, based his character on a notorious eighteenth century Dutch smuggler, Dirk Yawkins, who used the cave to hide tea, tobacco and spirits which he smuggled across from the Isle of Man. On one occasion, when landing contraband in the narrows of Kirkcudbright Bay, he was surprised by two revenue cutters. His only hope of escape seemed to be to try to pass the cutters by moving to the outside of the channel, but this made him vulnerable to the lethal broadsides of their guns. At the last moment, Yawkins changed course and steered through the narrow space between the two cutters. He was so close that he is said to have flung his hat on to the deck of one and his wig on to the other. To emphasise his defiance Yawkins hoisted a keg of spirits to the masthead and proceeded to outsail the slower revenue cutters.

Rather than storing alcohol in a cave, a more enterprising alternative was actually to produce it there. The illegal distillation of whisky was a popular pastime in parts of the Highlands up until the mid-nineteenth century, although the quality often left something to be desired. The remains of an illicit still can be found in a cave on the Isle of Mull, near the remote and now deserted township of CRAKAIG. Within the cave is a stone-built platform containing a basin some three feet deep, where the pot with the magic ingredients would be heated to evaporate off the alcohol. These operations clearly involved careful planning, because a turf dyke was built in front of the cave to hide any activity from passing ships at sea. The quality of this Mull whisky was such that it was said to have been popular not only locally, but also on neighbouring islands and even in Ireland.

Discovery of their activity within the Still Cave would not have been fatal to the illicit distillers, but the failure of others to remain inconspicuous would have brought lethal retribution. Prince Charles Edward Stuart made extensive use of caves when being hunted by government troops after the debacle at Culloden. He relied upon sympathisers to use their knowledge of the local country to hide him and thereby avoid capture and certain death. Amongst those who risked life and limb to help the Prince were the Seven Men of Glenmoriston, concealing him for four days in a cave above Coire Mheadhain, north of Glen Cluanie, Inverness. A month later, on 5th September 1746, after being passed from one group of supporters to another, he was hidden by Cluny Macpherson in a cave above Loch Ericht on the south slopes of **BEN ALDER**, Badenoch & Strathspey. This cave, known as Cluny's Cage, was well hidden and relatively spacious with an upper and lower level. After a week, word came that a French ship had arrived to take Charles to France. Following six days of hard walking over the hills he reached Loch nan Uamh, south of Mallaig, Lochaber, and sailed away to France and obscurity.

PRINCE CHARLES EDWARD STUART

The inhabitants of the ISLE OF EIGG were less successful than Bonnie Prince Charlie in their efforts to conceal themselves effectively and the consequences were disastrous. The clans of the MacLeods of Skye and MacDonalds of Clanranald were engaged in a long-standing and increasingly bitter feud which was steadily fuelled by attacks and counter-attacks. In 1577, in revenge for an assault on some of their clan, the MacLeods set sail for Eigg where the MacDonalds, expecting trouble, sighted the approaching war-galleys and decided to hide in the cave known as Uamh Fhraing (Cave of St Francis) in the south of the island. The cave has a very narrow entrance but widens out into a chamber seventy yards long by six yards wide. The MacLeods failed to find the cave, and contented themselves with burning and looting before departing.

As they were sailing away, the MacLeods spotted a MacDonald who had been sent out to discover what had been going on, and the galleys promptly returned. The MacDonald raced back to the cave to hide, but snow had fallen and the MacLeods were able to follow his footprints back to the cave. The narrow mouth to the cave made entry by any attackers suicidal, but also prevented the defenders from escaping. The MacLeods lit a fire and the smoke billowed into the cave, suffocating all the 400 or so inhabitants of the island.

Even more barbarous acts are reputed to have occurred in the caves below Bennane Head, near BALLANTRAE, Kyle & Carrick, during the fifteenth century. Over many years the area gained an unenviable reputation for the number of people who disappeared without trace. Extensive searches revealed nothing, but gruesome stories began circulating as to the fate of the missing persons. It was rumoured that they had been captured by an evil character by the name of Sawney Bean, and his extended family, who had become cannibals and eaten their victims. These bizarre stories eventually reached Edinburgh and the King was driven to action.

A huge manhunt was mounted in that part of Ayrshire, with several hundred men accompanied by bloodhounds. Sawney Bean and his family, said to number as many as 48 people including grandchildren, were tracked to the caves. There the horrified searchers discovered human limbs that had been dried or pickled in brine. A far cry from the message of peace and goodwill to all men spread by the early Christian missionaries. Retribution was quick. The prisoners were taken to Edinburgh where the men had limbs cut off and bled to death, whilst the women were burned alive. So much for the good old days!

One of SCOTLAND'S *most famous* LANDMARKS
– FINGAL'S CAVE –

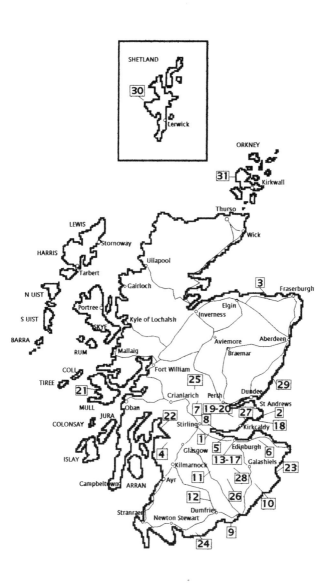

MAP 2 — HOME SWEET HOME

HOME SWEET HOME

Ref	Location	Description
1	Airth	Giant Pineapple
2	Anstruther Wester	Shell decorations on house
3	Banff	Duff House: legal wranglings
4	Bishopton	Misleading inscription date
5	Blackness	House of the Binns
6	Bolton	House of La Belle Stewart
7	Comrie	Earthquake house
8	Culross	House of the Evil Eye
9	Cummertrees	Unsuccessful holiday resort
10	Denholm	Text House
11	Douglas	James Gavin's lintel
12	Drumlanrig	Drumlanrig Castle
13	Edinburgh	Cannonball House
14	Edinburgh	Carving of boy's head
15	Edinburgh	House lost at cards
16	Edinburgh	House won at golf
17	Edinburgh	Deserted Dwellings
18	Elie	Lady's Tower
19	Falkland	Marriage lintels
20	Falkland	Inscriptions praising King
21	Gribun (Mull)	Rock that crushed a house
22	Helensburgh	Hill House
23	Kirk Yetholm	Gypsy palace
24	Kirkcudbright	House: Art Nouveau mosaic
25	Lawers	Lady of Lawers House
26	Linkumdoddie	Willie Wastle's wife's house
27	Lower Largo	Alexander Selkirk's house
28	Manor Valley	Black Dwarf's cottage
29	Montrose	Water-tower
30	Papa Stour	Maiden's Stack
31	Skara Brae	Stone Age houses

HOME
SWEET
HOME

SMALL *is* BEAUTIFUL

Given the basic need for shelter, houses are
the earliest permanent structures built by
man, but it is rare to find dwellings more
than a few centuries old still surviving.
This makes the oldest houses to be seen in
Scotland very remarkable indeed; in fact,
they are unique in northern Europe, being
all of 5000 years old – an age unlikely to be
matched by today's houses.

By the beach at SKARA BRAE, Orkney,
there are houses which were part of a Stone
Age settlement, dating from about 3000
BC. The outstanding state of preservation of
a number of these dwellings is due to their
being covered by drifting sand from
Neolithic times until they were exposed by
a storm in 1850. The typical house is about
twenty feet square with rounded corners. The
walls were up to ten feet high, probably
with wooden rafters, and a turf roof. In the
final phase of development the six houses
were linked by a passageway and then covered by a fragrant mixture of ash, dung and
bones. This at least had the advantage that
the inhabitants could find their way home
in the dark by smell. The shortage of wood
meant all the furniture was made of stone
and it is still possible to see beds, cupboards

and even dressers that were designed and built in the Stone Age. Unlike today's furniture such items were virtually indestructible. No doubt fashions in Neolithic times lasted for decades rather than days. The cramped conditions in these houses meant it was a major advantage for their inhabitants to be small.

However, by the eighteenth century, lack of height was seen as a distinct handicap, as David Ritchie, upon whom Sir Walter Scott based his character the *Black Dwarf*, knew only too well. This unfortunate man was born around 1740 and lived to be about seventy. He was only about forty inches in height and, having severely misshapen legs, was unable to wear shoes. He ended up propelling himself around with a long pole. Being considered a freak of nature, he was generally treated with suspicion, hostility or derision and it is hardly surprising that he is supposed to have had a black temper. The house which David Ritchie shared with his sister and where he spent the last nine years of his life, is near the hamlet of **MANOR** in the Manor Valley, Tweeddale. He insisted they lived separately and he had his own door. The special 'dwarf' door made for him can still be seen.

DECORATED HOUSES

Doorways and front walls are often of interest for their curiosity value. Since they are seen by everyone calling at a house, they have proved a popular means of conveying particular messages. A fashionable custom was for the couple living in a house to have their initials carved in the stone lintel above the door. Not surprisingly these are known as marriage lintels and a number can be seen, particularly in former small burghs such as those in North East Fife. **FALKLAND**, North East Fife, has an especially good collection. A stone now incorporated into a house front in Sharp's Close, bearing the initials 'IG' and 'AW' and the date '1659' was originally the marriage stone of John Geddie and Ann Wallace.

A sad story lies behind the lintel of James Gavin, whose trade as a tailor is shown by the scissors carved on his lintel in **DOUGLAS**, Clydesdale. In a barbaric act, his own scissors were used to cut off his ears because of his Covenanting activities. He was then banished to the Barbados penal colony in 1684. He subsequently returned home and the lintel is part of a memorial on the site of his former house.

EXAMPLES *of* LINTELS *in* EDINBURGH.

Flattery was the motive behind some wall inscriptions on houses, especially if they were visible to powerful neighbours. This is most apparent in **FALKLAND**, North East Fife, where residents opposite the Royal Palace blatantly curried the King's favour and seem to have become a bit carried away in their gushing praise. In 1610, Nicoll Moncreif had his wall inscribed: *'Al Praise to God And Thankis To The Most Excellent Monarche Great Britane, Of Whose Princelie Liberalitie this Is My Portioune.'*

KING JAMES VI

Not to be outdone, his next door neighbour commissioned an inscription which proclaimed: *'God Saif Ye King of Grit Britain, France, and Irland, Our Soveran. For Of Our Liberality This House Do I Edify.'* The reference to France is surprising. It could suggest that the householder's grasp of history was shaky; or that there was a gross excess of wishful thinking about James VI's ambitions and abilities when he became King of England as well as Scotland in 1603; or it may recall the fact that James VI's mother, Mary Queen of Scots, married the Dauphin and, for the brief period between his succession and his death, she was also Queen of France.

Some of the most entertaining inscriptions were never intended to be taken too seriously by their creators, although they can puzzle or even mislead the unwary. At Formakin House near **BISHOPTON**, Renfrew, the date 1694 and the initials 'DL' are cut in a crest above a gateway. Since the buildings date from the early twentieth century, this, to say the least, is very strange. The key to the mystery are the letters 'DL', which stand for 'Damned Lie' and reflect the cheeky humour of the owner, John Augustus Holms, a Paisley stockbroker and art enthusiast.

Artists have long been attracted to the delights of **KIRKCUDBRIGHT**, Stewartry. In the first few decades of this century the town was well known for its colony of artists, of whom the best known were Edward Hornel and Jessie M King. Both produced work in the 'Glasgow Style', with its strong Art Nouveau influence. Jessie M King specialised in book illustrations, with wispy damsels wandering through strange landscapes. Over the door of the house in which she lived and worked with her husband, E A Taylor, there is an unusual mosaic panel recording this fact, in appropriate 'Glasgow Style' typography.

The outstanding exponent of Art Nouveau was Charles Rennie Mackintosh. His masterpiece is the Glasgow School of Art, beneath the foundation stone of which is a manuscript decorated by Jessie M King. Mackintosh also applied his flair to domestic buildings and Hill House at **HELENSBURGH**, Dumbarton, is his distinctive creation. The house is unusual not only for its style, but also because Mackintosh designed all the furniture, fittings and decor as well. The outside may be rather austere, but inside it is an inspired combination of geometric

patterns, decorative detail and scattered touches of colour.

Not quite in the Mackintosh mould, but nonetheless entertaining for its detail, is a house at **DENHOLM**, Roxburgh, which has earned itself the name 'Text House'. Its façade is covered with various profound thoughts and exhortations, such as '*All was others: all will be others*' and '*Tak tent in time, ere time be tint*'. This was the brainchild in 1910 of a colourful local medical practitioner, Dr John Haddon. He is reputed to have suggested that a person could live on two gooseberries a day, but although he was a vegetarian, it seems such ideals were readily forgotten if someone else offered to treat him to a meaty meal.

Whether Dr Haddon was partial to seafood is not recorded, but the idea of covering a house front with seashells would probably have appealed to him. The unusual decorative patterns made by seashells on a house in **ANSTRUTHER WESTER**, North East Fife, date from the nineteenth century and were the trademark of a local eccentric, Alexander Batchelor. His obsession with shells extended to decorating one of his rooms in the harmonious tones of cream and brown shells. He maintained his distinctive house-style right up until the end, by providing a shell covered coffin for his own burial.

SHAPELY HOUSES

Sometimes the keeriosity value of a house stems from the unusual shape of the building itself, rather than just from the patterns on its walls. Some designs can have sinister connotations, although the so-called 'House of the Evil Eye' at CULROSS, Dunfermline, does seem to have been unjustly named. The two windows in the Dutch gable certainly look like eyes, but it is over-dramatic to see evil in them.

A better bet for discovering dark deeds associated with a domestic dwelling is the House of the Binns near BLACK-NESS, West Lothian. This house was owned in the seventeenth century by the controversial General Tam 'Bluidy' Dalyell, who became notorious for the allegedly cruel way he helped to crush the Covenanters. According to his enemies, he was in communication with the De'il (Devil). It was noted that not only did his name begin with a 'D' and end in 'L' but it was also pronounced to sound like his supposed mentor. Since both Tam and the De'il were fiery characters, they are said to have had frequent rows. After one such occasion, the De'il is reputed to have threatened to blow down Tam's house. To prevent this Tam had strong walls built, pinned down by turrets at each corner. This gave the house the distinctive shape which is still evident today.

GENERAL TAM DALYELL

A curious house also with a distinctive shape, known as the Lady's Tower, stands on the sea cliffs at ELIE, North East Fife. It is cylindrical and was built as a summer house for Lady Jane Anstruther in the eighteenth century. She liked to bathe in the sea near her house but, in those more modest times, she was reluctant to be seen by the local populace. To discourage prying eyes, a bell-man was sent around the village warning the locals to stay away from the tower whenever she went swimming. No doubt publicising the event in this way turned it into a challenge for some of the more resource-ful members of the local community and meant she was guaranteed a clandestine audience.

The daughter of Thorvald Thoressen would have been delighted to welcome secret visitors to her small tower. About seven hundred years ago she was confined by her father to a sea stack off **PAPA STOUR**, Shetland Isles, in order, he claimed, to protect her virtue. One particularly enterprising suitor, skilled in the art of rock-climbing, is said to have scaled the stack and helped her to escape. Since then the rock, at the entrance to Housa Voe, has been known as 'Maiden's Stack'.

Another unusual house associated with water is an octagonal tower at **MONTROSE**, Angus. This is an elaborate nineteenth century water tower that was built by the local council to house a cistern to supply water to the town. It has now been con-verted into a rather distinctive place to live and should especially appeal to anyone whose political views can be described as wet.

It is one thing to live in a former water tower, but quite another to live in a pineapple. In fact Scotland boasts what must surely be the world's biggest pineapple. This enormous fruit, about fifty feet tall, can be seen near **AIRTH**, Falkirk, on top of a building erected in 1761 as a garden retreat for the fourth Earl of Dunmore. It formed the centrepiece of the walled garden at Dunmore Park. The Pineapple was flanked by hot-houses, whose chimneys can be seen cleverly disguised as classical vases. It is quite possible that real pineapples were cultivated here, given the eighteenth century interest in exotic horticulture. Fortunately this improbable structure has now been saved – an unusual example, perhaps, of Pineapple preserve – and is available to rent as a holiday house.

HOUSES *of* MISFORTUNE

The collapse of a house is likely to have disastrous consequences for anyone inside, but there have been some remarkable cases of survival in such circumstances.

In 1861, two tenements in the High Street, **EDINBURGH**, collapsed, killing 35 people. Rescuers were surprised to hear sounds of life coming from under the rubble. As they dug, they could hear the muffled cries of a boy trapped underneath. To spur his rescuers on he shouted, 'Heave awa' chaps, I'm no dead yet'. These words have been immortalised by being carved, along with a boy's head, above the entrance to Paisley Close.

TENEMENTS *off* EDINBURGH'S HIGH STREET
– MYLNE'S SQUARE –

In the late eighteenth century, at **GRIBUN**
on the Isle of Mull, a newly-wed shepherd
and his wife were less fortunate. The house
where they were spending their wedding
night was situated right below a line of
cliffs. During the night an enormous boulder broke away and crashed down on the
cottage. For a brief moment they may have
felt the earth had moved for them, but sadly
the house was destroyed and they were
killed. The boulder was too heavy to move
and remains where it fell that tragic night.

The earth did literally move at **COMRIE**,
Perth & Kinross, and the town even has its
own Earthquake House. In 1789 an earthquake shook the town, which is situated right

on the Highland Boundary Fault. Further tremors occurred periodically, reaching a peak in 1839 when there were twenty in 24 hours. These were felt to be moving times locally and in 1869 a small building was erected just outside the town to house equipment for recording earth tremors. Needless to say this was soon followed by a cessation of seismic activity, but few people will be sorry to see this house remain unused.

It was military, not seismic, activity that caused concern to the residents of Cannonball House, at the upper end of Castle Hill in **EDINBURGH**. Embedded in the west wall of the house is a cannonball which is reputed to have been fired from the castle when it was being besieged by the Jacobite army in 1745. If so, the inaccuracy of the shot must have raised serious doubts about the competence of the castle's gunners.

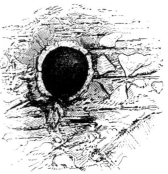

CANNON
BALL
*embedded in
the* WALL
in CASTLE
HILL

Sometimes the houses remained untouched by outside threats, although their residents were wiped out. Disease was usually the unseen hand behind this type of tragedy. An eerie example of this can be experienced in Mary King's Close, which lies under the present City Chambers off the Royal Mile in **EDINBURGH**. This close was originally eleven storeys high, linking the High Street with the Nor' Loch below. In the early seventeenth century, bubonic plague struck the city and all the residents of the close, one of whom was a Mary King, succumbed to the epidemic. Afterwards people moved back into the area, but stories of ghostly manifestations meant that Mary King's Close was first abandoned and then eventually sealed off. The part of the close above the level of the High Street was flattened and in 1811 the City Chambers were built over it, leaving a fascinating time-warp down below.

It is still possible to see the old houses, with their original front doors, including a peep-hole, a wooden-seated toilet, deserted rooms with their fireplaces, old iron hand-rails and gutters. There is a bakery with its oven, a wine store, and a butcher's shop with iron hooks still in the ceiling. Ghosts from the past never seem far away in the dimly lit shadows of Scotland's mini Pompeii.

In contrast to such grime and dinginess from the past, other places planned their future around bright lights and frivolity – but disaster struck just the same. At CUMMERTREES, Annandale & Eskdale, the problems were of a financial nature. Between 1890 and 1910 efforts were made by two local men, John Bell and Joseph Burnie, to transform the area between Cummertrees and the small fishing village of Powfoot into a major holiday resort. They had returned home after making money building houses on Merseyside, and set about developing a fifty acre site with houses, boarding houses, Hydro Hotel, boating lakes, bowling green, tennis club, and village hall in a style that reflected their experiences in England rather

than their own Scottish roots. The plans
depended on a sea wall, but it was never
built. Shifting tidal channels plus high costs
meant the enterprise was doomed. Cummertrees may never have fulfilled the aspirations
of its developers and is only a pale shadow
of its intended glory, but it has left in
Scotland an incongruous legacy of typically
English red brick and mock Tudor houses.

Escalating costs were always a potential
for financial disaster and a recipe for disputes
between builders and clients. Generally, the
higher the costs, the larger the house, the
more powerful the client, and the greater
the scope for lengthy litigation when parties
fell out with each other. William Adam
designed and supervised the building of
Duff House near BANFF, Banff & Buchan,
for Lord Braco. Work started in 1730 and the
house has been described as 'swaggering,
vainglorious and intimidating' – characteristics it seemed to share with its owner.

Adam intended to flank the main house
with pavilions. However, these were never
built, because a long and bitter disagree-
ment broke out between client and architect
over costs. The way both parties entered
into the project was destined to cause
trouble. No proper contract was drawn up,
no cost estimate was given and work even
started before the design was agreed. When
a bill for £2500 was received for the cost of
the carved capitals above the columns on
the front of the house, Lord Braco, so to
speak, hit the roof. He accused Adam of
overcharging and legal wranglings dragged

on until 1748. Adam won the case, but it did him little good – the strain contributed to his death shortly afterwards. Lord Braco was so embittered that he refused to live in the house and even took to closing the blinds on his coach when he passed by.

Another house on a grand scale which caused its owner financial palpitations was the palatial mansion at **DRUMLANRIG**, Nithsdale. It was completed in 1690 and certainly impressed Daniel Defoe, who described it as 'a palace so glorious, gardens so fine, and everything so truly magnificent'. The costs were also magnificent and did not impress the owner, William Douglas, first Duke of Queensberry. He was said to have been ruined by the expense.

Someone rather less pretentious than the Duke of Queensberry, but who also made an impression on the writer Daniel Defoe, was Alexander Selkirk. His adventures provided the inspiration for Defoe's classic book, *Robinson Crusoe*. Selkirk went to sea and became sailing master on the ship, 'Cinque Port'. In September 1704, when in the South Seas, he tactlessly quarrelled with the ship's captain, who promptly marooned Selkirk on the island of Juan Fernandez. When eventually rescued in January 1709, he was

found to be wearing clothes made of goat skins. In 1885 a statue of Selkirk, wearing his trendy goat skins, was erected on the site of the cottage where he was born at **LOWER LARGO**, North East Fife.

Whereas Defoe was able to romanticise Selkirk's adventures, the hapless wife of Willie Wastle held no romantic appeal for Robert Burns. She lived at the appealingly named **LINKUMDODDIE**, Tweeddale, in a cottage between Broughton and Moffat. The house no longer stands, but the site until recently was marked by a keeriosity in its own right – a tall rusty pole beside the road.

Robert Burns' well-known roving eye for the lassies found nothing to detain it in Linkumdoddie and his description of Willie's wife is scathing:

> *She has an ee, she has but ane,*
> *The cat has twa the very colour;*
> *Five rusty teeth, forbye a stump,*
> *A clapper tongue wad deave a miller;*
> *A whiskin beard about her mou,*
> *Her nose and chin they threaten ither ...*

In addition, she had:

> *Ae limpin leg a hand-breed shorter;*
> *She's twisted right, she's twisted left,*
> *To balance fair in ilka quarter:*
> *She has a hump upon her breast,*
> *The twin o' that upon her shouther.*

Not surprisingly, Burns concludes: *'I wad na gie a button for her!'*

ROBERT
BURNS

At the other extreme in the beauty stakes was the Duchess of Lennox, known as La Belle Stewart, and a former mistress of Charles II. In 1682 she bought Lethington House near BOLTON, East Lothian. She left it to Lord Blantyre, on condition that the house was renamed 'Lennoxlove' in memory, she claimed, of her love for her husband.

Although most of us may not be aware of it, the Duchess's physical charms are probably very familiar to us. In fact it can be said that she is held in a different person's hands every day. For she and money have become synonymous and she is well known through her modelling activities. Before her reputation is completely damned, it should be pointed out that it is her likeness rather than her physical person that is widely traded. To coin an explanation, she was the model for the figure of Britannia which appeared on British one penny coins until decimalisation and still appears on the 50p coin.

Whereas Britannia became the symbol of British national pride, Lennoxlove House is associated with a challenge to Scottish pride. The house is at the centre of a four hundred acre park, enclosed, it is said, in response to a comment made by the future James II of Britain (VII of Scotland), that Scotland was so lagging agriculturally that not even four hundred acres were enclosed. Anxious to prove James wrong, the Duke of Lauderdale, who owned Lennoxlove, promptly had four hundred acres enclosed by a high stone wall.

The absence of a garden wall was the least of Sir Laurence Dundas' worries, for he had the distinction of losing a house. In the end he finished up with one house for the price of two – a poor financial deal arising from an equally poor deal with his cards. What is now the Royal Bank of Scotland building on the east side of St Andrew Square, **EDINBURGH**, was designed as a magnificent private house for him in 1772. In a rash moment, he lost it on a bet in a game of cards with General John Scott. He was only allowed to keep his own home after agreeing to build the General a new house nearby in Dublin Street.

The ROYAL BANK *of* SCOTLAND – ST ANDREW SQUARE

HOUSES *of* GOOD FORTUNE

What Sir Laurence Dundas lost at cards, John Paterson won at golf. Large winnings from golf are not a recent phenomenon, although they are now usually associated with the professional game. In the seventeenth century, however, a shoemaker and talented amateur golfer, John Paterson, won a small fortune from a golf match. He partnered the Duke of York – later James VII and II – when they beat a pair of English noblemen at golf on Leith Links. There must have been a lot of pride at stake, because the betting stakes were such a size that Paterson was able to build himself a new house from his share of the winnings. This house, known as 'Golfer's Land', was built in the Canongate, in **EDINBURGH**.

Paterson was clearly proud of his golfing prowess, because in addition to 'I hate no person' (anagram of his name), he displayed a new coat of arms, showing a dexter hand holding aloft a golf club, and a new motto 'Far and Sure' on the front of his house. Such words will strike a chord with golfers everywhere. It might have been appropriate for the house to be approached by a long 'drive', but unfortunately it was right on the street. The plaque and motto can be seen on the site where Paterson's house formerly stood.

'A NOTED
GOLFER'
by KAY

HOUSES *of* FORTUNE TELLERS

An invaluable talent for anyone indulging in a bet is to be able to foretell the future. Fortunately for bookmakers there are few who have this ability. Gypsies are traditionally associated with fortune telling and their Scottish centre was in **KIRK YETHOLM**, Roxburgh. A former local laird is said to have been saved by a gypsy while fighting in Europe. In gratitude he made part of his land available to the gypsies. Among those settling in the area were the family claiming descent from the royal line. One of the best-known was Esther Faa Blyth – gypsy queen until her death in 1883. She lived in a simple cottage which she called her palace. 'The

Palace' can still be seen above the door.

Though she does not seem to have had gypsy blood, the 'Lady of Lawers', who lived on Loch Tayside from about 1650, was a renowned fortune-teller. The ruins of her house remain at LAWERS, Perth & Kinross. Known for the accuracy of her prophecies, she foretold a number of local happenings including the fate of the local church, local economic problems and the demise of the Campbells of Glenorchy. She is said to have foretold the clearance of local people from the land thus: 'The land will first be sifted, then riddled of its people ... the jaws of the sheep will drive the plough from the ground ... the home-steads on Loch Tay will be so far apart that a cock will not hear its neigh-bour crow.' All came to pass.

As for the Campbells of Glenorchy, she foretold: 'The Earldom will not descend beyond a grandson in one line ... in time the estates of Balloch will yield only one rent and then none at all ... the last laird will pass over Glenogle with a grey pony leaving nothing behind.' All have come true, the last in 1948 when the final laird sold Kinnell House and left in a trap pulled by a grey pony.

It is said that the only prophecy still to be fulfilled predicts: 'The time will come when Ben Lawers will become so cold that it will chill and waste the land around for seven miles.' What might this refer to? With concerns about global warming, rather than cooling, it might seem unlikely, but no doubt this was the initial reaction to all her other prophecies – yet the cynics have been proved wrong.

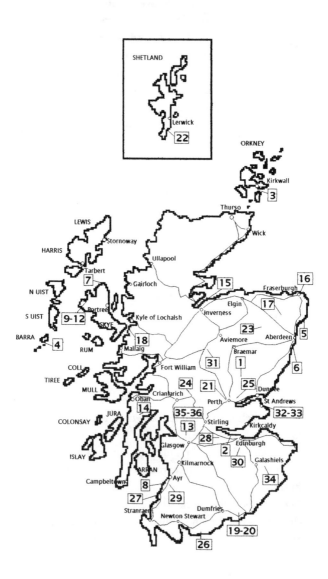

MAP 3 — HOLDING THE FORT

HOLDING THE FORT

Ref	Location	Description
1	Balhary	POW camp
2	Blackness	Ship-shape castle
3	Burray	Block ships
4	Castlebay (Barra)	Kisimul Castle
5	Cruden Bay	Original Castle Dracula
6	Dunnottar	Scottish Regalia hidden (1652)
7	Duntulm	Careless prisoner
8	Dunure	Spit-roasted cleric
9	Dunvegan	War of One-eyed Woman
10	Dunvegan	Feasting to excess
11	Dunvegan	MacLeod's Table
12	Dunvegan	Fairy Flag
13	Faifley	Foundations of decoy city
14	Fincharn	Wedding night blaze
15	Fort George	Impregnable fortress
16	Fraserburgh	Castle turned lighthouse
17	Fyvie	Figure of trumpeter
18	Glenelg	Barracks
19	Hoddom	Beacon platform
20	Hoddom	Watchtower
21	Huntingtower	Maiden's Leap
22	Isle of Mousa	Broch
23	Kildrummy	Traitor's gold
24	Killin	Beheading pit
25	Kinfauns	Rhineland castles
26	Kirkcudbright	Laird's Lug
27	Lendalfoot	Castle of 'false' Sir John
28	Linlithgow	Vomitarium
29	Maybole	Carved heads of gypsies
30	Penicuik	Copy of King Arthur's Round Table

HOLDING
THE
FORT

Castles are both our most enduring and most endearing reminders of past strife and unsettled times. Scotland is castle country par excellence. Castles fulfilled a number of functions and although they were primarily residences for feudal lairds and their households, they also served as courthouse, prison, bank and even hotel. The higher a laird's social standing, the larger his retinue and hence also his castle.

Political instability and a habit of settling disputes by force meant that both the site and design of castles reflected the need for security. Thomas Kirke, in 1679, summed up the situation in Scotland when he wrote: 'Indeed all the gentlemen's houses are strong castles, they being so treacherous one to another, that they are forced to defend themselves in strongholds.'

People living in the countryside had to hope they could obtain protection within their local castle in times of trouble. Residents of burghs were in a potentially safer position since every burgh's charter allowed it to construct a defensive wall. Owing to the cost few burghs were able to afford a stone wall. Some relied on earthen ramparts or ditches for protection, but many lacked any form of worthwhile defence at all. The most impressive stretch of town wall to survive in Scotland is at **STIRLING**. Here the stone walls are over ten feet high, contain gun loops and retain their corner bastions. They were built in 1547-48, 'at this peralus tyme of neid, for resisting oure enemies of England'.

SIEGES

Whereas today many castles are besieged by tourists, in the past visitors hoping to gain entry often had less friendly intentions. Those castles near the English border generally experienced the most excitement, thanks to the popular pastime of cross-border raiding. Since to be forewarned is to be forearmed, it was prudent to keep a sharp look out for impending trouble. The tower-house at **SMAILHOLM**, Roxburgh, for example, has a seat for a watchman and a recess for his lantern, because the Border Laws required that 'in war and in peace, the watch to be kept on the house-heads; and in war the beacon in the fire-pan to be kept and never fail burning, so long as the Englishmen remain in Scotland'.

A burning beacon of a different and more peaceful sort adorns the sixteenth century tower-house at Kinnaird Head near **FRASERBURGH**, Banff & Buchan. The castle's site and height proved ideal for conversion into a lighthouse in 1787. The lantern housing is the converted cap-house of the tower's spiral stair.

At **HODDOM**, Annandale & Eskdale, the castle still has its original beacon platform and is also notable for its unique early-warning system. At the first sign of hostile activity, signals were sent to the castle from a watchtower, known as Repentance Tower, on nearby Trailtrow Hill. The tower, like the castle, was built by John Maxwell in the sixteenth century. It is so named because the word 'Repentence' is carved above the door. Apart from indicating that spelling came second to fighting in local priorities, the name appears to reflect John Maxwell's remorse at destroying a ruined chapel in order to provide stones for his tower.

Border skirmishes were generally short, sharp affairs, unlike the drawn-out sieges which were the lot of some of the larger castles when faced by English forces. Edward I of England seemed to enjoy a good siege. The stronger the castle the greater the challenge he found it. Consequently the siege of the castle at STIRLING in 1304 must have had special appeal and made up for a previous occasion when the castle's garrison heard he was coming and promptly ran away. For three months Stirling Castle withstood the batterings from 13 siege-engines hurling stones, lead and anything else to hand. Threatened by starvation, the defenders un-der Sir William Oliphant wanted to surrender, but Edward refused to accept this and insisted that the castle be 'struck with his War Wolf, and those within defend themselves from the said War Wolf as best

A SIEGE ENGINE *in the* TIME *of* EDWARD I.

QUEEN
ELEANOR,
WIFE *of*
EDWARD I

they can'. The colourfully named War Wolf was his latest siege weapon, which he wanted to try out in action. The theatrical effect was enhanced by cutting a window in a nearby house to allow the English queen and her entourage to watch the spectacle.

Two years later, Edward I's son, later Edward II, was also displaying the family fondness for sieges. In 1306, he besieged the castle at **KILDRUMMY**, Gordon, where the defenders were led by Sir Nigel Bruce, brother of Robert Bruce. The strong walls helped the defenders to resist all the English attacks until the castle succumbed to treachery. The smith in the castle, a man named Osbarn, was secretly in the pay of the English and was able to end the siege by using a piece of red hot metal to set fire to the granary. With its food gone, the garrison was forced to surrender and Sir Nigel Bruce was hanged at Berwick. Osbarn, however, received his just desserts. His reward, negotiated previously with the English, was to have as much gold as he could carry. What he had not bargained for was that he would receive the gold in liquid form, poured down his throat!

The spectacularly sited castle at **DUN-NOTTAR**, Kincardine & Deeside, also received the attention of English forces when it was besieged for eight months by Cromwell's General Monk in 1652. The prize was the Scottish Regalia, retained in Scotland following the Union of the Crowns in 1603, and known to have been moved to Dunnottar for safekeeping. The Regalia, consisting of crown, sceptre and sword, were smuggled out of the castle and through the English lines. This is reputed to have been achieved by lowering the Regalia by rope to the seashore, where the servant girl from the nearby Kinneff Manse was waiting. She regularly searched the shore for seaweed and shellfish to eat and was a familiar figure to the besieging army. She hid the Regalia in her basket and carried them past the English troops to the safety of Kinneff Church (*see* chapter 4, 'Sacred Sites').

One technique used to besiege a castle was to undermine the walls. An interesting and extremely rare example is the siege mine and countermine under the castle at **ST ANDREWS**, North East Fife. These were constructed in the siege of 1546-47. Sappers from the attacking Catholic forces under the Earl of Arran cut the tunnel through solid rock. This Herculean task resulted in a gallery, some six and a half feet high, going under the castle ditch to a mine-head from where a series of smaller tunnels were to be driven under the walls. The Protestant defenders, aware of what was going on, desperately sought to intercept the tunnel by building their own countermine. After several false starts, evident as shafts sunk within the castle, and much wasted excavation work, they eventually broke through into the mine. The castle's garrison was, however, forced to surrender some time later after coming under bombardment by French ships.

DARK DEEDS

The laird of a castle was responsible for enforcing law and order, which gave him the

ST ANDREWS CASTLE

power of pit and gallows over his fellow citizens. The castle at Finlarig near **KILLIN**, Stirling, is unique in Scotland in retaining its beheading pit, as an alternative to the more popular gallows tree. Clearly Black Duncan Campbell, who built the castle, liked to keep 'ahead' of his rivals.

A number of castles still have their dungeons or pits, but the bottle shaped one at **ST ANDREWS**, North East Fife, is particularly impressive: 24 feet deep and carved out of solid rock. Many of those incarcerated in these dark, dank holes were no doubt victims of a miscarriage of justice; but some, such as Hugh MacDonald, who died a prisoner in the dungeon of Duntulm Castle, Isle of Skye, brought trouble on themselves.

Hugh had ambitions to become Chief and sought to fulfil them by devising a scheme to have his cousin, Donald Gorm, the eighth Chief, murdered. The plan was to invite Donald Gorm to a party where he would be killed by an assassin named Martin. But in his haste to execute this deed, Hugh became careless in the extreme. He muddled the invitation to his Chief with the detailed plans explaining to Martin what his role was to be. Not surprisingly, Donald Gorm did not take too kindly to reading these proposals to have himself killed. He promptly had Hugh arrested and imprisoned at Duntulm. To show his hospitality he fed Hugh generous quantities of meat. The catch was that it was well salted and no drink was provided. This ensured that Hugh suffered a lingering death from thirst.

Someone else who suffered during imprisonment in a castle was a certain Alan Stewart. He, however, was an unfortunate victim of a gross injustice in 1570. He was unlucky enough to hold the title of Commendator of Crossraguel Abbey in Ayrshire, a position which gave him rights to use the land – something that Gilbert Kennedy, fourth Earl of Cassillis, desired for himself. To attain his own ends, Kennedy kidnapped Alan Stewart and brought him to his castle at DUNURE, Kyle & Carrick. To persuade the Commendator to sign over his rights, Kennedy literally turned the heat on. He tied his hapless victim to a spit and started to roast him, whereupon the Commendator decided to co-operate. When doubts were expressed as to the validity of this signature, Kennedy again kidnapped the Commendator and proceeded to repeat the treatment until the latter agreed that his previous signature had been freely given.

Another castle associated with dark deeds

is New Slains Castle near CRUDEN BAY, Banff & Buchan. The building is a strange, foreboding ruin perched on the edge of sea cliffs and is said to have been Bram Stoker's inspiration for the Castle Dracula of his spine-chilling vampire stories. Bram Stoker came regularly on holiday to the area and had a second home in the nearby village of Whinnyfold. On a dark stormy night, the sea boiling around the rocks below the castle, it takes little imagination to see it as 'the very place where he [Dracula] has been Un-Dead for all these centuries ... full of strangeness of the geological and chemical world'.

BATTLE *of the* SEXES

Most castles have been the scene for a battle in some form or another, but one common to nearly all of them has been the battle of the sexes. This was particularly true of Carleton Castle near LENDALFOOT, Kyle & Carrick. One of the castle's former owners, the 'false' Sir John Cathcart of Carleton, seems to have borne a particular grudge against the fair sex. Despite this he had no problem in finding someone to marry him – but never for long. His policy was to dispatch his current wife to eternity by pushing her over the nearby sea cliffs. He did this on seven occasions, but his resourceful eighth wife proved to be a bride too far. She seems to have become suspicious about the fate of her predecessors for, when the time came, she reacted first and threw Sir John over the cliffs instead.

The nearby castle at MAYBOLE, Kyle &

Carrick, was also the scene of an unhappy marriage. The wife of the Earl of Cassillis, who lived in the castle, went off, willingly it is thought, with a gypsy, Johnnie Faa and his gang. They were pursued and captured by the Earl and his men. The gypsies were hanged and, to ensure his wife never forgot this episode, the Earl had the heads of the gypsies carved in stone and placed around the castle tower.

Another stone figure commemorating an unhappy end to a love affair can be seen on top of one of the towers on the castle at FYVIE, Banff & Buchan. This figure is said to be of Andrew Lammie, the Laird's trumpeter, who courted Annie Smith, daughter of the local miller. The miller, however, had higher social ambitions for his daughter – the Laird himself. He therefore forbade her to see Andrew. But when the Laird sent the trumpeter away from the castle, this was all too much for Annie. Shortly after, she died of a broken heart.

A lot of trouble might have been saved if Andrew and Annie had simply eloped from Fyvie. Dorothea, daughter of the first Earl of Gowrie, certainly found this to be the case in the sixteenth century. In the process she also found that she had a talent for long-jumping. The occasion arose when she heard her mother coming up the stair towards the room in one of the towers of her parents' castle at HUNTINGTOWER, Perth & Kinross, where she was being entertained by her lover, John Wemyss of Pittencrieff. To escape detection, and at a height of sixty feet above the ground, she successfully leapt across a ten foot gap to the adjacent tower where her own room was. Her mother, failing to find Dorothea where she expected, went back to her daughter's room and found her in her own bed. She apologised for her unwarranted suspicions, but the next night Dorothea eloped with her lover.

Fyvie Castle was not alone in being the scene of a romance jeopardised by the actions of the Laird, and ending in a death. In the distant past, local lairds traditionally enjoyed many rights which would be looked upon with amazement today. One of these was the option to spend the wedding night with the bride of one of his tenants. This might well have appealed to the laird, but it was, not surprisingly, less popular with the bride and groom. On one occasion the Laird of the castle at FINCHARN, Argyll & Bute, decided to exercise this right. No doubt his thoughts were racing on ahead and it was some time before he noticed that the bridegroom was not at the wedding feast in the bride's house. He ordered a search to be mounted and this led to the discovery that his castle was ablaze. Suspecting the bridegroom was responsible, the Laird ventured forth to find the young man. However, the latter was waiting for him – and to ensure that the Laird would be unavailable for proceedings later that night, the bridegroom killed him.

Another ancient custom, but one which has now returned to favour, was for couples to live together before marrying. This was traditionally known as hand-fasting and was described by Martin Martin in his book

Description of the Western Isles, published in 1703. He noted:

> *It was an ancient custom in the Isles that a man take a maid to be his wife and keep her for the space of a year without marrying her; and if she pleased him all the while, he married her at the end of the year, and legitimised her children; but if he did not love her, he returned her to her parents.*

Since the women do not seem to have been consulted in all this, there was the distinct possibility that they or their family would feel snubbed and rejected if they were 'returned'. This provided the seeds for conflict as the people of the Isle of Skye discovered.

Around 1600, Donald Gorm MacDonald hand-fasted with Margaret MacLeod in the MacDonald stronghold of Duntulm Castle on Skye. During the course of the year Margaret damaged her eye and was 'returned' to the care of her brother, Rory Mor, at the MacLeod fortress of DUNVEGAN Castle, Isle of Skye. To add insult to the injury, Margaret was sent back on a one-eyed horse, led by a one-eyed groom and accompanied by a one-eyed dog. Donald Gorm clearly no longer had his eye on Margaret. The MacLeods were incensed by the way the sister of their Chief had been treated and a two year conflict broke out, known as the War of the One-eyed Woman.

By contrast, in the Northern Isles, a dispute between rival families also threatened to lead to conflict, but it was resolved amicably. The *Orkneyinga Saga* tells how, in 1153, a

MOUSA BROCH *on the* ISLAND *of* MOUSA – SHETLAND

character by the name of Erland abducted
Margaret, mother of Earl Harald Maddason,
from Orkney to Shetland and 'persuaded' her
to set up home with him in the broch on the
island of MOUSA, Shetland Isles. It was not
long before Harald discovered where they
were and he laid siege to the broch. However,
Erland must have made the most of his time
with Margaret because she agreed to marry
him and battle was averted.

The broch itself is a spectacular feature in
its own right, being the best-preserved of
these unique Scottish fortified structures. They
were built about 2000 years ago and are
concentrated in the north and northwest of
the country. Brochs are circular shaped towers
with double walls that slope inwards towards
the top. The one at Mousa is about 43 feet
high. Within the hollow drystone walls is a
stair leading to six galleries. The outer wall
lacks windows and entry is by a single door.

WITHIN *the* WALLS

The walls of a castle provided the defenders with a protective shield to resist the actions of an enemy, and these vitally important features came in a range of shapes and sizes. Perhaps the most unusually shaped walls are those around the castle at **BLACKNESS**, Falkirk, which looks for all the world like a stone galleon on the shore waiting to be launched into the water. Local tradition attributes this distinctive outline to a promise made to King James V by Archibald Douglas, who was Lord High Admiral of the Scottish navy. Concerned about English naval power, which was threatening Scotland, James was anxious to strengthen his navy. To impress the King, Douglas promised James that he would build a warship which the English would find unsinkable. True to his word, he built the ship-shaped castle at Blackness.

Castle-like walls are not always what they may first appear to be. Perched on crags above steep wooded hillsides and overlooking the Perth/Dundee road near **KINFAUNS**, Perth & Kinross, are two castellated towers. Their function was decorative, not defensive, since they were built as part of the romantic movement in the 1820s. They were designed to stimulate the imagination into comparing this stretch of the River Tay with the River Rhine near its confluence with the Moselle! The Tay grapes are conspicuous by their absence, but the Tayberries are tasty.

Elsewhere, too, walls were not always what they might seem. In a few castles the expression 'walls have ears' is literally true. A particularly impressive example of this exists at MacLellan's Castle in **KIRKCUDBRIGHT**, Stewartry. This imposing structure was not so much a tower-house as a political 'power-house'. It was completed in 1582 for Sir Thomas MacLellan, a local property magnate and the Burgh Provost. He was able to keep his ear politically attuned thanks to an effective bugging device. Incorporated into the conspicuous fireplace in the Great Hall was an inconspicuous 'Laird's Lug', or hole, through which he could eavesdrop on his visitors' conversations.

The walls of Kisimul Castle in **CASTLEBAY**, Isle of Barra, were put to a novel use by the chief of the MacNeil clan, whose stronghold this was. The MacNeils had a high opinion of their own importance, even if this view was not shared by their neighbours. After the Chief had eaten his main meal, it is recorded that a herald would appear on the battlements and announce to anyone who cared to listen: 'Hear, ye people, and listen, ye nations! The MacNeil of Barra having finished his dinner, all the princes of the earth are at liberty to dine!' The proclamation would have been made in Gaelic, but little of the flavour seems to have been lost in translation. It is also known on Barra that the then Chief declined Noah's offer of a lift in the Ark because the MacNeil of Barra had a boat of his own.

It was not just the MacNeils who took their eating and drinking seriously. Thomas Kirk, visiting Scotland in the seventeenth

century, noted the Scots' generous hospitality
and a liking for the occasional liquid refreshment of an alcoholic kind. He observed that
'it's their way of making you welcome, by
making you drunk'. This seems to have been
amply borne out by some of the spectacular
feasts held at DUNVEGAN Castle on the Isle
of Skye by one of the MacLeod chiefs, Rory
Mor. According to an English translation
from the Gaelic verses by the bard Niall Mor
MacMhurich:

> *Six nights I had been at the Dun. It was not
> fallacious entertainment I received .... We had
> inebriating ale and a blazing fire .... In his
> royal court drinking is not a dream. To his
> numerous company he is plentiful and hospitable
> .... We were twenty times drunk every day, to
> which we had no more objections than he had.*

Obviously a great time was had by all. It is
easy to understand the need for a vomitarium,
or small room like the one off the banqueting
hall in the Palace at LINLITHGOW, West
Lothian, to where those who indulged thus
could retreat and be sick, often deliberately, in
order to be able to resume eating and drinking.

The Dunvegan area had previously been
the setting for a spectacular feast in 1560. The
MacLeod Chief of that time, Alasdair Crottach,
had been at a feast in Holyrood Palace in
Edinburgh. He had boasted that in Skye he
could eat in grander surroundings than those
to be found at Holyrood. His room was bigger,
his table much larger, the candlesticks were
taller and the lighting more beautiful. His

bluff was called and a lowland lord insisted on visiting Skye to see for himself. The MacLeod Chief's credibility was at stake if he was not to become a laughing stock. Alasdair Crottach rose to the challenge by providing an open-air banquet. The table was the flat-topped hill of Healaval Mor, near DUNVEGAN, and it has been known ever since as MacLeod's Table. The candlesticks were his clansmen holding aloft flaming torches. Natural lighting was provided by the moon and the stars. The visitor seems to have gone away duly impressed.

Perhaps the most famous table of all time was the Round Table of King Arthur. It is thought that Arthur was a Romano-British leader of a highly mobile cavalry force who successfully resisted the invading Anglo-Saxons in the sixth century. The West Country of England has tried to claim Arthur for its own, but the only area where there is unambiguous evidence for his presence is Scotland. Of the twelve major battles recorded as being fought by Arthur, the Wood of Caledon, which is clearly in Scotland, is the only one where even the general location is beyond dispute.

Recent reasoned research by American scholars has suggested not only that his Round Table was located in central Scotland, but that an exact copy of its design can still be seen. In reality, it appears to have been neither wooden nor a table, but a curious stone structure, located near Stenhousemuir. The confusion is attributed to a monk's incorrect translation from a twelfth century French text. Arthur, it is suggested, used not a 'round table' but a 'tabled rotunda', inside which he would meet with his knights. This strange building, twenty-two feet high, was known locally as Arthur's O'on (reflecting its oven-like shape) and is first mentioned in a ninth century document which refers to ' ... a round house of polished stone on the bank of the River Carron'. Despite being unique in Europe and of great antiquarian interest, it was demolished in 1743. Fortunately an exact replica of this structure was built in 1763 by Sir John Clerk on top of the stable block at Penicuik House, near PENICUIK, Midlothian, where it can still be seen.

While King Arthur had his magic sword, Excalibur, the chief of the Clan MacLeod had the magical Fairy Flag or Bratach Sith, still to be seen at DUNVEGAN Castle, Isle of Skye. It is said to have been given to the fourth chief, Iain, by his fairy wife when she had to return to her homeland. To this worn and faded piece of silk, with its gold thread and crimson spots, is attributed the power to rescue the Clan from disaster. There is a potential difficulty in that the flag can only be waved a maximum of three times for this purpose. It has been used twice to good effect – once to save the MacLeods' cattle from a serious disease at a time when cattle were the mainstay of the local economy and once against the MacDonalds at the Battle of the Spoiled Dyke near Trumpan Church (*see* chapter 4, 'Sacred Sites'). Cynics have suggested that should the flag be used again, the most likely consequence is that it would fall to pieces.

'The CASTLE is dead – long live FORTIFICATIONS!'

The age of the stone-built castle in Scotland lasted from the twelfth to the seventeenth century. It came to an end owing to a combination of greater political stability and improved military hardware. More powerful artillery meant castle walls ceased to offer an effective defence against attack, but the need to be able to provide this declined as firmer central government control brought greater internal peace. These developments allowed private resources to be devoted increasingly to concerns of comfort, privacy and aesthetics and the mediaeval castle evolved into the country house.

Thereafter the construction of defensive installations became the prerogative of central government. Following the Jacobite rebellions of 1715 and 1745, the government embarked on a military building programme in the Highlands. This included barracks, still visible at **GLENELG**, Lochaber, and **RUTHVEN**, Badenoch & Strathspey (completed 1721). The 1745 uprising had revealed defects in the existing small forts and barracks such as Ruthven, since they were captured by the Jacobites.

To prevent a repetition of such events, an impressive and impregnable new fortress was built at **FORT GEORGE**, Inverness, to house 1600 soldiers. According to General Wolfe, victor over the French in Quebec, it was 'the most considerable fortress in Great Britain'. Even Doctor Johnson had to admit that it 'well deserves the notice of the traveller'. Its massive curtain walls have bastions projecting from the corners to provide comprehensive covering fire and its magazine was built with walls thick enough to withstand a direct hit from a mortar bomb, making it virtually impregnable to contemporary weapons. It is a unique monument to Georgian military engineering and one of Europe's most spectacular artillery fortifications, being virtually unchanged since it was completed in 1769.

Its formidable defences were never required and this clearly disappointed Lord Ligonier when he was Commander-in-Chief of the British Army. He desperately wanted the French to attack the fort: 'I shall be extremely glad that they would do it because I look upon the fort to be impregnable against any force that could be sent against it.'

Subsequent defensive military installations were built in response to external, not internal, threats to security. A number of particularly interesting and unusual defensive features remain in Scotland as legacies from World Wars I and II. In order to prevent enemy submarines entering the important naval anchorage at Scapa Flow in Orkney and attacking British warships, a number of block ships were sunk in World War I to try to close the easternmost approach channels. Despite this, on 14th October 1939, a German submarine (U-boat 47) managed to avoid the block ships, enter Scapa Flow undetected and escape the way it came, after sinking the battleship 'HMS Royal Oak'. To ensure this never happened again, the islands were then linked by a solid causeway, built by Italian prisoners-of-war and named the Churchill Barriers. Several of the original block ships can still be seen beside the Churchill Barriers to the north and south of the island of BURRAY.

A rare legacy from World War II is a virtually complete prisoner of war camp near BALHARY, Perth & Kinross. This camp has somehow escaped the fate of nearly all the other such establishments, which were cleared away as soon as they were no longer required after the war ended.

One of the more extraordinary, and ingenious, episodes in the last war was the construction of decoy cities as part of a plan code-named 'Starfish'. These decoy sites on hills bordering the Clyde Valley were designed to lure German bombers away from the strategically important and heavily populated shipbuilding areas along the Clyde and towards concentrations of anti-aircraft guns. The decoys replicated the dockland areas by a string of imitation street lights controlled from a central switchboard. This was activated on the imminent arrival of enemy bombers and there was also the facility to start false fires. The complex was very extensive and included sites in the Campsie Hills, at Condorrat near Cumbernauld, and on the Isle of Bute. There are still remains of building foundations in the Kilpatrick Hills to the north-east of FAIFLEY, Clydebank.

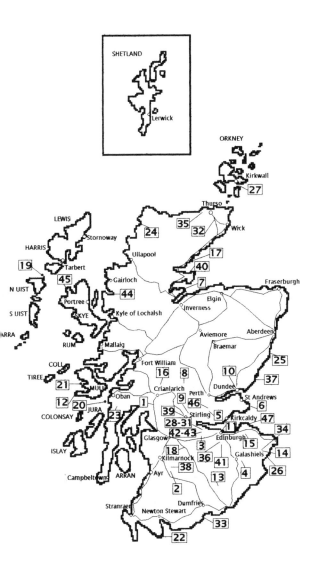

SHETLAND

Lerwick

ORKNEY

Kirkwall

27

Thurso

35 32

Wick

LEWIS

Stornoway

24

Ullapool

17

40

HARRIS

19

Tarbert

45

Gairloch

7

Fraserburgh

N UIST

44

Elgin

Portree

Inverness

Aberdeen

S UIST

SKYE

Kyle of Lochalsh

Aviemore

ARRA

RUM

Mallaig

Braemar

25

COLL

Fort William

10

37

TIREE

16 8

Dundee

21

MULL

Crianlarich

Perth

St Andrews

12

Oban

9

46

6

20

JURA

39

Stirling

5

Kirkcaldy

47

COLONSAY

1

23

28-31

11

34

42-43

Glasgow

Edinburgh

15

ISLAY

18

3

36

41

14

Kilmarnock

4

26

38

Campbeltowns

13

ARRAN

Ayr

2

ISLAY

Stranraer

Dumfries

Newton Stewart

33

22

MAP 4 — SACRED SITES

SACRED SITES

Ref	Location	Description
1	Ardlui	Pulpit Rock
2	Auchinleck	Misnumbering of the Ten Commandments
3	Bathgate	Cutty Stool
4	Bowden	Laird's Loft
5	Cleish	Sanctuary crosses
6	Crail	Arrow marks on church
7	Cromarty	Laird's Loft
8	Dull	Stone sanctuary cross
9	Dunblane	Broken cross
10	Dundee	Head displayed on church tower
11	Edinburgh	Letter 'S' sanctuary markers
12	Eilean nam Ban	Women's Island
13	Eskdalemuir	Tibetan pagoda
14	Fogo	Laird's Loft
15	Garvald	Jougs
16	Glen Cailleach	Tigh nam Bodach (House of the Old Man)
17	Golspie	Laird's Loft
18	Hamilton	Echo – Duke of Hamilton's Mausoleum
19	Isle of Berneray	Parliamentary Church
20	Isle of Luing	Alex Campbell's warnings
21	Isle of Ulva	Parliamentary Church
22	Isle of Whithorn	Church on site originally below high water
23	Killineuer	Skeletal handprint
24	Kinlochbervie	Parliamentary Church
25	Kinneff	Church where Scottish Regalia was hidden

Ref	Location	Description
26	Ladykirk	Church provided by James IV
27	Lambholm	Italian Chapel
28	Linlithgow	Scene of James IV's apparition
29	Linlithgow	Royal coat of arms
30	Linlithgow	Window with red lobster
31	Linlithgow	Window portraying innocence of childhood
32	Mybster	Meeting House with spelling mistake
33	New Abbey	Sweetheart Abbey
34	Polwarth	Refuge for Sir Patrick Hume
35	Reay	Jougs
36	Roslin	Apprentice Pillar
37	St Vigeans	Loch with water-horse
38	Sorn	Jougs
39	Stirling	Divided church
40	Tain	St Duthac's Chapel
41	Temple	Inscription about Kirk Session controls
42	Torphichen	Sanctuary stone
43	Torphichen	Disputed Laird's Loft
44	Torridon	Preaching site
45	Trumpan	Church burned down in mass murder
46	Tullibole	Outdoor Communion table
47	Whitekirk	Church burned by suffragettes

SACRED SITES

FOUNDERS

Churches have been founded for a variety of motives, not all entirely selfless. Their founders have sometimes been attracted by thoughts of self-glorification or of buying their way into Heaven. Nevertheless, some churches were established as genuine acts of thanksgiving. King James IV, for example, narrowly escaped drowning when crossing a ford during a sudden spate on the River Tweed. As a thanks-offering to the Virgin Mary for his safety, he paid for a church to be built nearby at **LADYKIRK**, Berwickshire.

Churches were often dedicated to a female saint or to the Virgin Mary, but they were rarely founded by a woman. A spectacular exception was the great monastic church of Sweetheart Abbey at **NEW ABBEY**, Nithsdale. It was founded by Lady Devorguilla in 1273. She was the devout and devoted wife of John Balliol and the church was her memorial to him, along with Balliol College at Oxford which she also endowed. As a permanent reminder of her much loved husband, Devorguilla had his heart embalmed. She kept it in a casket and when she died his heart was buried with her in front of the high altar. As a result the Abbey became known as 'Dulce Cor' or Sweetheart.

UNUSUAL SITES

An even more romantic and remarkable couple are associated with a remote site in GLEN CAILLEACH, Perth & Kinross. They are known in Gaelic as Am Bodach (the Old Man) and An Cailleach (the Old Woman) and their memorial is a far cry from the grandeur of an abbey. Instead it is a lowly stone-built structure that acts as a house (Tigh) and is known as Tigh nam Bodach.

Each year it is the scene of the re-enactment of a special and ancient custom, the origins of which are lost in the mists of time, but seem to stem from pagan rather than Christian worship. Every summer the Cailleach, her husband, three children and a baby are brought out from the house and each autumn they are carefully bedded down for the coming winter. The Cailleach must be treated with great reverence and respect: to do otherwise would bring misfortune.

Who or what then is this mysterious Cailleach who has given her name to the glen in which she lives? She is 18 inches high and has a slim neck and small flat-topped head. In reality she and her family are cylindrical water-worn stones. The Cailleach herself is remarkable because she is thought to be an extremely rare representation of the Mother Goddess, the all-powerful earth-deity, who was worshipped by our early ancestors. The livestock, which she used to watch benignly over and helped to protect if she was well treated, are no longer moved up into the glen for the summer, but the traditional spring and autumn ceremonies of opening and closing the Cailleach's house are, fortunately, still continued by the local stalker.

Another unusual site for open-air worship, and also associated with a stone, is on the banks of Loch Lomond to the south of ARDLUI, Dumbarton. In this case the stone – called 'Pulpit Rock' – is huge, being an enormous 50 foot high boulder that was used as an open-air church in the nineteenth century. There is a hole which was cut out of the rock in 1825 in order to provide a vestry and pulpit for the minister from Arrochar. Services were held at the stone until 1895 when a permanent church was built at Ardlui.

Sometimes people had to worship outside, even when there *was* a church available. In some cases this was because the church was so popular that it was completely full. Such an event happened sufficiently often at TULLIBOLE, Perth & Kinross, for a small area of grass to be built up and enclosed by a trench to provide a simple table for serving Communion. In other cases it was because the worshippers refused to use the existing church. When the Church of Scotland split in 1843, many people broke away to form

their own Free Church congregations. Landowners often denied them sites on which to meet, so services were frequently held by the shore where landlords had no jurisdiction. One such preaching site, tiered in small stone-built terraces, can be seen at Am Ploc, on the shore near TORRIDON, Ross & Cromarty.

At the ISLE OF WHITHORN, Wigtown, the only site that members of the newly formed Free Church could obtain was below high water mark. Not to be deterred, they brought in material to infill part of the harbour and then built their church upon it. The church has stood there ever since.

Another church thought at one time by its parishioners to have water below it, is at ST VIGEANS, Angus. Local tradition held that the stones for the church had been carried into position by a kelpie or water-horse – a beautiful but malevolent water-spirit which frequented a loch beneath the church. Between 1699 and 1763 no Sacrament of the Lord's Supper was held in the church and the view developed that if the Sacrament were to be re-introduced, the church and its congregation would sink into the underground loch. When a communion service was re-introduced, the congregation decided the minister must have taken leave of his senses. Instead of entering the church, they chose to watch from the safety of a small mound a hundred yards away. The predicted disaster failed to occur and local fears of the kelpie soon vanished.

UNEXPECTED BUILDERS

In some areas it was a shortage of money rather than land that prevented churches from being built. This was particularly true in many parts of the Highlands where poverty was endemic for much of the nineteenth century. The government, concerned for the inhabitants' spiritual needs – if not always their physical ones – provided grants for church building. Churches funded in this way became known as Parliamentary Churches and 32 were built between 1823 and 1835. They were constructed to a standard design drawn up by Thomas Telford, the road, bridge, harbour and church builder extraordinaire. Examples include the churches on the ISLE OF BERNERAY, Western Isles; ISLE OF ULVA, Argyll & Bute; and KINLOCHBERVIE, Sutherland.

What is probably the most unusual of all the churches in the Highlands and Islands was built not by Parliament but by prisoners. It was constructed during World War II by Italian prisoners-of-war who were building the Churchill Barriers to prevent submarines from entering the naval anchorage at Scapa Flow (*see* chapter 3, 'Holding the Fort'). The church is still known as the Italian Chapel and is on the small island of LAMBHOLM, Orkney.

It was built out of two Nissen huts, using whatever material came to hand. From such an unpromising beginning a really beautiful church has been fashioned. There is a superbly crafted wrought iron rood screen and paintings of the Madonna and Child on the chancel wall behind the altar table. Plasterboard has been skilfully painted to resemble tile and brickwork. On the outside, the outlines of the building's humble origins have been hidden behind an impressive façade of an archway supported by cement pillars and a belfry. The original designer – Domenico Chiocchetti – returned to Orkney in 1960 to restore the paintings, but the wet and windy climate provides a hostile environment for conserving this moving masterpiece.

Whilst the north of Scotland has its touch of Italy, the south has experienced an even more exotic influence with a touch of Tibet in ESKDALEMUIR, Annandale & Eskdale. A pagoda with Tibetan lamas is, to say the least, an unexpected sight to come across in the south of Scotland. It is Europe's largest Buddhist temple and the only one in the western world built in the traditional Tibetan style. The Samye Ling community of Tibetan Buddhists has been established here since the 1960s. This may not be the Himalayas, but Eskdalemuir can still give the impression of being remote and is suitably cold in winter to make the monks feel at home.

PLACES *of* SANCTUARY

Whereas the Tibetan monks have constructed their own place of sanctuary in Eskdalemuir, other people have sought sanctuary in existing churches. Fugitives and outcasts reaching a sanctuary were supposedly safe from pursuit. A determined pursuer, however, could ignore such niceties. Robert the Bruce killed the Red Comyn in the sanctuary of Greyfriars Church in **DUMFRIES**. In turn, his wife and daughter were taken from the sanctuary of St Duthac's Chapel at **TAIN**, Ross & Cromarty, and handed over to Edward I in 1306.

To prevent such violations, some sanctuaries were physically protected. The one centred on the Preceptory of the Knights of St John at **TORPHICHEN**, West Lothian, was patrolled by the Knights to stop sanctuary from being broken. The centre of the sanctuary is in the churchyard, where it is marked by a stone pillar about three feet high, on which is incised a cross. The area covered by the sanctuary extended for a radius of one mile and the boundaries are still delimited by three of the original refuge stones.

In other instances the limit to the safe ground associated with the sanctuary is actually marked by a cross. At **DULL**, Perth & Kinross, one of the original large stone crosses can be seen close to the parish church; and at **CLEISH**, in the same district, the sanctuary stones around the perimeter of the church-yard are marked by a series of small incised crosses.

Concerning serious crimes, fugitives were guaranteed the right to sanctuary only until a fair trial could be arranged. They could not escape the consequences of their action if guilty. For less serious misdemeanours such as debt, sanctuary seems to have been granted for as long as needed. The sanctuary offered by the Abbey of the Holy Rood, **EDINBURGH** became a haven for debtors from the 1530s

HOLYROOD ABBEY CHURCH – EDINBURGH

until 1880 when imprisonment for debt was abolished. Ironically perhaps, a solicitor was the last debtor to seek refuge in the Abbey. Amongst those using this sanctuary to avoid their creditors were the exiled Charles X of France and the writer, Thomas de Quincey.

These 'Abbey Lairds', as they became known, could leave the safety of the sanctuary – marked today by the letter 'S' inserted into the road at the east end of the Canongate – without fear of being arrested, but only on a Sunday. One minister, heavily in debt, used to walk to his church to take the Sunday service before returning to the safety of the Abbey sanctuary. What any of his parishioners to whom he owed money thought of this can only be guessed at.

The church at **POLWARTH**, Berwickshire, was also used as a refuge when in 1685 Sir Patrick Hume sought safety within it. He was being hunted by the soldiers of Charles II, not for owing money, but because he had been accused of involvement in a plot to kill the Duke of York. He protested his innocence, but to avoid arrest he remained hidden in the vault of the church for a month, depending on food passed to him through the window bars each night by his twelve year old daughter. He subsequently fled to the Netherlands, but returned in 1688 when William of Orange became king.

Another church that in the seventeenth century successfully hid the hunted from the hunter was at **KINNEFF**, Kincardine & Deeside. The hunters were once again soldiers, but the hunted in this instance was the Scottish Regalia – Crown, Sceptre and Sword. After being smuggled out of Dunnottar Castle (*see* chapter 3, 'Holding the Fort') the Regalia were hidden under the floor of Kinneff Church for nine years. They were regularly brought out for cleaning by the minister, Mr Grainger, and his wife, until 1660 when secrecy ceased to be required with the Restoration of the Monarchy.

The KIRK SESSION

There were many unfortunate people who, far from seeking sanctuary in their local church, only attended under extreme pressure when they were summoned to appear before the Kirk Session. In their cases, the church offered anything but a refuge. The Session comprised

the minister and kirk elders, who were elected
by the congregation. Its functions included
supervising social matters such as education
and poor relief, as well as the more juicy moral
issues such as Sabbath breaking, drunkenness
and sexual misbehaviour. The Kirk Session
was given the power to enforce laws covering
these matters when they were incorporated
into the category of civil offence. Since civil
courts could often impose more severe
sentences, people generally elected to suffer
the embarrassment and humiliation of
punishments imposed by the Kirk Session.
Some of the Kirk Session records read, at
times, like the goings-on reported in the
more sensational of today's tabloid newspapers.

Not surprisingly, the Session instilled fear
in many, but occasionally individuals hit back
by drawing attention to what they felt were
unreasonable actions by the Kirk Session. One
such person was Elizabeth Hunter. On the
memorial stone to her brother-in-law, Charles
Hitchener, in the churchyard at **TEMPLE**,
Midlothian, the inscription records that she
had been 'prevented by the members of the
Kirk Session of Dalkeith from paying this
tribute of gratitude and respect to the memory
of the deceased in their burying ground where
the body is interred'.

The Session's usual treatment of miscreants
was to obtain a public statement of repentance
and then subject them to indignities for a
given number of Sundays. These included
confinement by the neck in jougs – iron collars
attached to the outside of the church wall –
usually near the door so as to be in full view

of everyone entering the church. Jougs can still be seen on the walls of several churches, including **REAY**, Caithness; **SORN**, Cumnock & Doon Valley; and **GARVALD**, East Lothian.

An alternative punishment was to spend the service seated on the stool of repentance, conspicuously located at the front of the congregation. To compound the humiliation, offenders sometimes were compelled to wear sackcloth and this performance could be repeated for several months. 'Cutty stools' or stools of repentance have become extremely rare, although one that was formerly in the High Kirk at **BATHGATE**, West Lothian, is now in the town's Bennie Museum. It is unusual in that it has a double seat which allowed any unmarried couple who had transgressed together to be rebuked together.

Children too did not escape punishment on this particular cutty stool. Troublesome tearaways were bent over the stool and birched by the church beadle. No doubt to the relief of both young and old in Bathgate, this awesome stool has not been used for many decades.

This preoccupation with the serious side of life was at the expense of the more frivolous and entertaining. There was no light relief during the long hell-fire sermons, but there was one place that managed to avoid such oratory. This was the chapel above the Duke of Hamilton's mausoleum at **HAMILTON**. On its completion in 1856, it was discovered to have an incredible echo that could last for up to 15 seconds. Such accursed acoustics were too much for any minister, even one obsessed with the sound of his own voice.

VIOLENCE *in* CHURCH

Although the more fiery orators might lambast their parishioners for succumbing to the sins of the flesh, such violence was only verbal. Unhappily, despite their reputation as places of peace, churches have sometimes witnessed physical violence and been the scene of brutal murders. In some cases the victim's demise has sprung directly from his work on the church itself. For example, the best known feature of the chapel at ROSLIN, Midlothian, is the ornate 'Apprentice Pillar', which, tradition has it, was carved by an apprentice in his master's absence. The quality was so impressive that the master mason, on his return, is said to have killed the apprentice in a fit of jealousy. There is a carved head in the south-west corner which is reputed to be that of the unfortunate apprentice.

The head of a murder victim was also displayed on St Mary's Church, DUNDEE. In 1651, during General Monk's assault on the city, the church tower was used as a refuge by local people and soldiers under General Lumsden. They were safe in their retreat until smoke from burning straw forced them to surrender – a case of being overcome by holy smoke. General Lumsden's head was then cut off and placed on top of the tower, where it is said to have stayed for 150 years.

Military activity also damaged, albeit slightly, the Cathedral at DUNBLANE, Stirling. In February 1746 government forces, under the notorious Duke of Cumberland, were billeted at Dunblane during their pursuit of

Bonnie Prince Charlie's Jacobite army. The animals used for transporting the army and its provisions were kept in the Cathedral grounds under armed guard to prevent them from being stolen. During the night one of the sentries accidentally discharged his gun and the musket ball hit and broke the stone cross on the Cathedral's west gable. The cross remains broken to this day.

Rather more than minor damage was done to the church at TRUMPAN, Isle of Skye, in 1578. In fact it was totally destroyed during an act of mass murder. The MacDonalds of South Uist, in revenge for the massacre of their clansfolk on the Isle of Eigg by the MacLeods (see chapter 1, 'Cave-Dwellers'), crossed the Minch and set fire to the church, which was full of people. Their attack was reported to the Chief of the MacLeods at Dunvegan Castle and he hurried to the area with reinforcements. The MacDonalds' planning had overlooked the fact that their attack coincided with high tide. This meant that when they came to escape, they found that their war galleys had been left stranded by the falling tide. Unable to retreat, they were all killed in the ensuing fight. Their bodies were buried by tumbling a stone dyke down on top of them and this bloody encounter became known as the Battle of the Spoiled Dyke.

Another church associated with the horrors and disasters of battle is St Michael's at LINLITHGOW, West Lothian. In 1513, James IV attended evening service before setting off on his ill-considered invasion of England, which ended so disastrously at the Battle of Flodden. While James was kneeling at prayer, a strange apparition suddenly stepped out of the shadows. This, plus what happened next, is described by Sir Walter Scott in *Marmion*:

> *Stepped from the crowd a ghostly wight*
> *In azure gown, with cinture white*
> *His forehead bald, his head was bare*
> *Down hung at length his yellow hair ...*
> *My mother sent me from afar*
> *Sir King, to warn thee not to war,*
> *Woe waits on thine array.*

Whether this strange vision was a ghost, or someone put up to the part by Queen Margaret in a desperate bid to dissuade her husband from embarking on such a reckless folly, is not known. Sadly, what is known is that James ignored the warning and both he and thousands of his supporters paid for this mistaken decision with their lives.

A ghostly warning was also delivered and ignored in the church at **KILLINEUER**, Argyll & Bute, but with less serious consequences. Stories that this ruined church on the south shore of Loch Awe was haunted encouraged the local tailor to boast that since he was so unconcerned, he would make a pair of trousers inside the ruins during the night. On the night in question the tailor had not long started on his task when he was interrupted by the sight of a ghostly hand rising out of a grave, and a weird voice enquiring if he could see the hand. The tailor, not to be scared off so easily, replied that he did, but he would continue to sew. After he had carried on for a while undisturbed, the peace was broken by the sight of a skull appearing from the grave, and the eerie voice asked if he could see the skull. A bit less confident this time, the tailor replied that he did, but would continue sewing. After several further such exchanges, which served to undermine the tailor's self-confidence, the whole skeleton appeared. This was all too much for the tailor and he fled, terrified. As he escaped through the door, a bony hand lashed out at him. He ducked and it missed him, but hit one of the stones by the door, leaving its ghostly imprint which is still visible to this day.

A different type of impression, also left as an indelible mark on a church wall, can be seen at **CRAIL**, North East Fife. It too has its origins in violence, but between men rather than with spirits. The marks are deep grooves made by archers sharpening their steel-tipped arrows. Up until the early eighteenth century, churchyards were regularly used for archery practice in response to various Acts of the Scottish Parliament which required that 'the younger men of every parish practise archery for an hour or two after Divine Service'.

DISPUTES *of* REPUTE

Fortunately disputes, which can occur for the most unlikely of reasons, do not always lead to bloodshed, even though feelings run high. Petty jealousies, for instance, can arise over apparently trivial matters, such as seating arrangements in church.

In principle everyone is supposed to be equal in the eyes of God, but this notion seems to have been lost on the more material-minded within a congregation. An imposing pew to sit on became a much sought-after status symbol. Even better was to build a loft or gallery, since this was thought to emphasise the elevated social standing of the funder. Hence such structures were popular with the local lairds and also allowed them to enjoy the comfort of their own private fireplaces. This ensured that they, at least, were warmed during, if not by, the minister's sermon. Impressive examples of laird's lofts, usually displaying the family crest, can be seen in places ranging from **GOLSPIE**, Sutherland, and **CROMARTY**, Ross & Cromarty in the north, to **BOWDEN**, Ettrick & Lauderdale, and **FOGO**, Berwickshire in the south.

Trivial as it may seem, lairds were not above disputing who was entitled to sit in the loft. Both the loft and church at **TORPHICHEN**, West Lothian, were built in the 1750s by the local laird, Henry Gillon. Never in his wildest dreams would it have occurred to the unfortunate Mr Gillon that he would be prevented from using his own loft. On completion of the church, Lord Torphichen, as the feudal superior, claimed it was his privilege to enjoy the comforts of the laird's loft, including the fireplace that Mr Gillon had specially built. Not surprisingly, Mr Gillon was incensed and took his case to the Court of Session in Edinburgh. Not only was justice slow – the case dragged on for seven years – but it seems to have been entirely absent as the court found

in favour of the absentee Lord Torphichen.
The crestfallen Mr Gillon had to resort to the
front row of the adjacent gallery.

Certain people seem to have been in dispute
with the world at large, rather than with any
particular individual. At Kilchattan's ruined
church on the ISLE OF LUING, Argyll & Bute,
a colourful character and staunch Presbyterian
by the name of Alex Campbell displayed his
wrath by means of written messages which he
engraved on stones and placed around the
churchyard. Few things met with his approval.
His dislikes included the Church of England,
his brother Duncan, George III, play-actors,
dancing schools, parasols and men with
whiskers. Still to be seen are his warnings
about the Judgment in store for those who
'meddle with this stone again' and for local
children who teased him, crying 'bald head!'

By contrast, St Columba's dispute seems
to have been with women at large. He banned
both women and cows from the Island of Iona,
apparently on the basis that 'where there is a
cow there is a woman; and where there is a
woman there is mischief'. It is interesting to
think that men were seen as the innocent
party so far as mischief was concerned. Thanks
to St Columba's prejudices, all women, even
the wives of lay workers on Iona, were accom-
modated on a small adjacent island, still
known as EILEAN NAM BAN (Women's Island),
Argyll & Bute.

St Columba's views about the female sex
would not have made him popular with the
Suffragettes during their campaign to persuade
Parliament to give women the right to vote.

He would, however, have been understandably saddened by their action in setting fire to the church at **WHITEKIRK**, East Lothian, in 1914. The whole interior was destroyed. Those responsible were never apprehended, but a note found by the church stated: 'By torturing the finest and noblest women in the country you are driving more women into rebellion .... Let McKenna, Asquith & company beware lest they break that last barrier.' On a happier note, the building was sensitively restored by Sir Robert Lorimer in 1917.

An earlier dispute had seen Parliament itself trying to increase its power. The English Parliament, in the guise of Oliver Cromwell, had fought a successful Civil War and over-thrown the King, Charles I. The King was, however, monarch of Scotland as well as of England, and the attempt by Charles II to regain the throne from a Scottish base led to Cromwell's army invading Scotland. The grandiose royal coat of arms inside St Michael's Church in **LINLITHGOW**, West Lothian, dates from this period. It was hastily purchased by the burgh council following the Restoration of the Monarchy in 1660. The councillors hit on this clever idea to demonstrate their new-found loyalty to the crown and thereby distract attention from their amicable relationship with Cromwell's forces during the previous ten years when the soldiers had been garrisoned in the town.

Split loyalties led to the physical division of the church of the Holy Rude, **STIRLING**, in 1656. Revd James Guthrie was a fiery Presbyterian, and at a time of bitter dispute between Presbyterians and Episcopalians, his views were too much for many of the towns-folk. As a result, not only the congregation, but also the minister and his assistant, split. Neither side wanted to incur the cost of building a new church, so a compromise was reached by building a wall across the middle of the church. The Presbyterians, led by Guthrie, retained the choir; and the Episcopalians, led by his deputy, Matthew Simpson, used the nave. This dividing wall was not removed until as recently as 1936.

ACCIDENTS *and* MISTAKES

Despite the care and attention devoted to religious handiwork, craftsmen still made some intriguing mistakes. Spelling often caused difficulties. For example, on a stone tablet above the door of the Meeting House about three miles south of **MYBSTER**, Caithness, the mason carved: 'BUILT by Superscription Anno Domini 1842', clearly confusing his super and subscripts. Uncertain as to the spelling of 'subscription', he sought help from the Bible. In St Mark 15:26, he found the word 'super-scription' and, assuming this was what he was looking for, he cut it into the stone. The error was discovered only after the building was completed. To try to rectify the situation, tar was used to cover the letters 'e' and 'r', and an attempt was made to convert the 'p' into a 'b'. The tar has been eroded by the weather, leav-ing the mistake permanently revealed.

Stone tablets are usually associated with Moses and in one of the church windows at

AUCHINLECK, Cumnock & Doon Valley, he is portrayed carrying the Ten Commandments. But his task is made unduly complicated by the fact that there are two with 'VI' on them.

Moses may have been a water-baby, but Prof. Sir Charles Thomson was a water-borne naturalist who made his name leading a scientific expedition in 'HMS Challenger' (1872-76). The voyage was designed to study the underwater life of the world's oceans and, though highly successful, it took its toll on the health of Sir Charles. He died six years later. In his memory a large stained-glass window, which included underwater scenes, was placed in the church of St Michael's, near where he lived in LINLITHGOW, West Lothian.

The window-artist may have known his own trade inside out, but he was clearly a novice on natural history. To his embarrass-ment, it was discreetly pointed out that he had made a mistake. Contrary to what was portrayed in the window, no self-respecting and uncooked lobster was a bright red colour. The artist's credibility was eventually saved by the lobsters themselves when one of their number, a new species, was caught off Australia and found to be a pinkish colour.

Another stained glass window in St Michael's Church recalls a tragic accident. It was erected by Dr Ferguson when he was the minister, in memory of his daughter, nine year old Esther. She died in 1888 from terrible burns, caused by her hair catching fire as she was drying it in front of the fire. The picture shows the Boy Samuel at prayer in the temple and portrays the innocence of childhood.

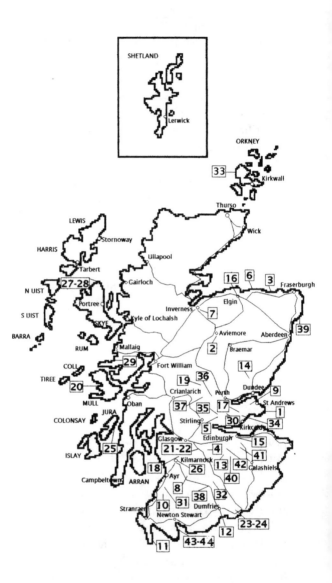

MAP 5 — DYING TO BE REMEMBERED

DYING TO BE REMEMBERED

Ref	Location	Description
1	Anstruther Easter	Gravestone with long name
2	Aviemore	Shaw Mor's gravestone
3	Banff	Stolen and re-cut effigies
4	Cambusnethan	James Weir's gravestone
5	Cleish	Boundary stone of lair
6	Cullen	Gravestone with name changed from Innes to Duff
7	Culloden	Battle graves
8	Cumnock	Sarah McLatchie's gravestone
9	Cupar	Covenanting gravestone
10	Dailly	John Brown's gravestone
11	Drummore	Lighthouse gravestone
12	Dumfries	Monument to cholera victims
13	Dunsyre	Covenanter's Stone
14	Eassie	Gravestone 'die and be forgot'
15	Edinburgh	Gravestone of Jean Stuart
16	Elgin	Gravestone of John Geddes
17	Falkland	Statue to Onesiphorus Tyndall-Bruce
18	Fenwick	James White's gravestone
19	Fortingall	Mound of the Dead
20	Gruline (Mull)	Major General Lachlan Macquarie's Mausoleum
21	Hamilton	Duke of Hamilton's Mausoleum
22	Hamilton	Covenanting gravestone
23	Hoddom	Gravestone of West African
24	Hoddom	Clockmaker's gravestone
25	Inverlussa (Jura)	Mary MacCrain's gravestone & longevity

DYING
TO BE
REMEMBERED

Scotland has a particularly rich and distinctive heritage of decorated seventeenth and eighteenth century gravestones. They are dominated by three main themes – emblems of mortality/immortality, biblical scenes and trade symbols. However, fascinating as these are, it is those stones which are distinctive for their unusual, quirky or even bizarre nature that probably provide the greatest curiosity value.

Humour on gravestones is usually unintentional, since epitaphs were closely vetted by the Kirk Session. For example, at Brechin in 1619:

> *The Session considering that monie abuses are admittat in making epitaphs be young men in this citie affixing on burial stanes anie thing they ples, partlie rediculous and partlie ontrew, ordain that no epitaph shall he put on any monuments without the approval of the session.*

Although the Kirk Session usually ensured that flippancy was censored, some humour has slipped through. Many of the funniest epitaphs that have been reported either seem to be apocryphal or are no longer legible. Nevertheless some gravestones encourage us to raise an eyebrow and even a smile, despite

being reminded of death.

En route to the GRAVE

Before being buried, the deceased had to be
carried to the graveyard. In rural areas where
roads were poor or non-existent, the corpse
might have had to be borne for several miles.
The weight of the coffin meant that the pall-
bearers required periodic stops for rest and
refreshment. Cairns, known as coffin-cairns,
were erected to mark such stopping places –
particularly impressive examples can be seen
near **KINLOCHMOIDART**, Lochaber.

At **MAWHILL**, Perth & Kinross, there is a
large flat stone, known as the 'Leckerstane'. It
is raised above the verge and was used for
resting coffins on. Its name is said to be
derived from 'Liquor Stone', since it was not
unknown for the pall-bearers to take a well-
earned dram or two to help them on their way.
Quite what effect this drinking may have had
on their subsequent sense of direction is best
left to the imagination.

LAIRDS *and* LAIRS

Following the Reformation, burial inside
churches was forbidden and everyone, not just
the wealthy, became entitled to a monument,
however humble. Needless to say, those with
money were often anxious to draw attention
to themselves. To ensure they were not
forgotten after their deaths, they were in the
habit of constructing grandiose places for
their burial. These generally took the form of

vaults or aisles adjoining the church.

The most extraordinary mausoleum of all
is to be seen at **HAMILTON**. It was built by
Alexander, 10th Duke of Hamilton, reputedly
a vain and pompous man, who considered
himself the rightful king of Scotland. As a
fitting memorial both to himself and to what
he considered his illustrious ancestors,
Alexander built what *The Gentleman's
Magazine* described as 'the most costly and
magnificent temple for the reception of the
dead that was ever erected – at least in Europe'.

Work started in 1845, but before it was
completed Alexander died in 1852. In
accordance with his eccentric wishes, his
body was embalmed and placed in an Egyptian
sarcophagus on a raised pedestal within the
burial vaults beneath the unfinished chapel.
The chapel was not finished for another four
years.

Less pretentious families acquired their
own lairs or plots in the churchyard. A rare
instance of a boundary stone for a family lair
can be seen on the graveyard wall at **CLEISH**,
Perth & Kinross. It proclaims, 'All to the
south of this belongs to Cleish Mill'. Graves
were often marked with head and foot stones.
The head markers began to be increased in
size so they could contain details of the
deceased. In the seventeenth century these
became increasingly ornate and richly carved.
On some stones the prime interest lies in
such carvings; on others the fascination
derives from the wording on the epitaph.

CAUSE *of* DEATH

Death can be brought about by illness, accident, war and murder. References to each can be found on gravestones and monuments. In the days before cleanliness was considered to be next to godliness, and drugs were virtually unheard of, outbreaks of diseases were a constant threat to whole communities. Plague held a particular terror in the Middle Ages and carried off large numbers of people. At FORTINGALL, Perth & Kinross, the mass grave of plague victims is opposite the church and is marked by a stone on top of Carn Na Marbh (Mound of the Dead).

During the plague of 1645-46 in the Perth area, Mary Gray and her cousin, Bessie Bell, decided to isolate themselves on the Lynedoch estate, owned by Mary's father. They were visited there by Bessie's lover, who brought them not only food but also, inadvertently, the plague. They were buried by a ford over the River Almond at Dronach Haugh, north of METHVEN, Perth & Kinross. Their grave is amongst trees and now protected by railings. Their story was taken to North America by emigrants and is remembered in the names of two hills near the town of Staunton, Virginia. These hills are called Mary Gray and Betsy Bell.

Mass outbreaks of cholera were also not uncommon. Such an epidemic broke out in DUMFRIES, Nithsdale, in 1832, and is commemorated by an imposing memorial in St Michael's churchyard to the 420 victims who were buried in a common pit.

Mass graves also result from wars. In Scotland such graves can be seen at CULLODEN, Inverness. This was the scene in 1746 of the last major battle fought on British soil. The Jacobite clans, under the disastrous leadership of Bonnie Prince Charlie, were slaughtered both during and after the battle by the government troops, under the notorious Duke of Cumberland. The fate of the clans is recalled by poignant references to their names on top of the graves.

The clans supporting the Jacobites were mostly but not exclusively Catholic and those on the government side were mainly Protestant. However, in the religious fervour of the previous century, Protestant slaughtered Protestant in what became known as the 'Killing Times'. Atrocities were committed by zealots from both the Episcopalian and Presbyterian sides.

When Charles II was restored to the throne, he tried to impose Episcopacy on Scotland, which was staunchly Presbyterian. Many, such as the Covenanters, actively opposed the introduction of bishops and an ecclesiastical hierarchy, along with the associated formal rituals. Covenanters refused to use the Established Church and took to worshipping at open-air conventicles. This was made illegal and government troops pursued them relentlessly, provoking retaliation and armed uprisings.

In 1666, after one such uprising had been crushed at Rullion Green, south of Edinburgh, a badly wounded Covenanter, John Carphin, tried to make his way home to Ayrshire.

THE BATTLE OF RULLION GREEN

Dying from his injuries, he sought assistance at the isolated cottage of Adam Sanderson. Having being given some sustenance, Carphin insisted on leaving but, shortly after, he collapsed and died on the slopes of Black Law hill. Sanderson respected his last wish and buried him further up the hillside within sight of the Ayrshire hills. To confuse any pursuing soldiers, and to stop them from removing the body should they find it, Sanderson carved cryptic lettering on the gravestone. In the nineteenth century this stone was moved to DUNSYRE, Clydesdale, and placed inside the church, where it still remains.

Perhaps the most moving of all the monuments to the Covenanters are those found in the Wigtown district of Galloway. They are also extremely unusual in that two

of the people commemorated were women –
18 year old Margaret Wilson and 63 year old
Margaret MacLachlan. These 'Wigtown
Martyrs' were sentenced 'to be tied to
palisades, fixed in the sand, within the flood-
mark of the sea and there to stand until the
flood overflowed them and drowned them'.
The older woman was tied to a stake further
out so that the sight of her drowning would
change the mind of the youthful Margaret
Wilson. Remarkably, the latter refused to
give in and was drowned proclaiming, 'I am
one of Christ's children. Let me go!' Their
graves can be seen in **WIGTOWN** churchyard,
where their ordeal is recorded in crude script
on Margaret Wilson's stone:

> *Murter'd for ouning Christ Supreame*
> *Head of his church and no more crime*
> *But not abjuring presbytry,*
> *And her not ouning prelacy.*
> *They her condemned, by unjust law,*
> *Of Heaven nor Hell they stood no aw.*
> *Within the sea ty'd to a stake*
> *She suffered for Christ Jesus sake.*
> *The actors of this cruel crime*
> *Was Lagg, Strachan, Winram and Grahame*
> *Neither young yeares nor old age*
> *Could stop the fury of their rage.*

Callousness seems to have known no
bounds and it was not uncommon to cut heads
and limbs off the bodies of Covenanters. At
CUPAR, North East Fife, a stone illustrates
that interred within the grave are not only the
heads of Laurence Hay and Andrew Pitulloch,

who 'suffered martyrdom' at Edinburgh in 1681, but also the hand of David Hackston who was 'most cruelly murdered' at Edinburgh in the previous year. At **HAMILTON** there is a stone carved with the heads of four Covenanters, who 'suffered' at Edinburgh in 1666. The words state:

> *Stay passenger, take notice what thou reads;*
> *At Edinburgh lie our bodies, here our heads,*
> *Our right hands stood at Lanark, these we want,*
> *Because with them we swore the Covenant.*

An even more gruesome scene is conjured up by the words on the stone of James White at **FENWICK**, Kilmarnock & Loudoun:

> *This martyr was by Peter Ingles shot.*
> *By birth a tyger rather than a Scot,*
> *Who, that his monstrous extract might be seen,*
> *Cut off his head & kicked it o'er the green,*
> *Thus was that head which was to wear a crown,*
> *A football made by a profane dragoon.*

It makes modern football hooliganism seem quite tame ....

Whether a killing is considered legitimate or an act of murder tends to depend upon who is doing the killing. This is apparent from the gravestone of Philip Kennedy who was killed, aged 35 years, on 19th December 1798. He is buried at **SLAINS**, Banff & Buchan. He was a local smuggler and one night, as he and his brother were moving smuggled goods, they were intercepted by Excise Officers. In the ensuing struggle Philip's skull was struck by a sword. Mortally wounded he struggled home and died shortly after. The Excise Man was subsequently tried for murder, but acquitted.

Those killed in their prime often died as a result of the work they engaged in legally. Coal-mining disasters have resulted in large losses of life, but one of the most tragic cases was that of John Brown, who is buried in the churchyard at **DAILLY**, Kyle & Carrick. In 1835, a roof-fall at the Kilgrammie Pit trapped him underground for 23 days 'in utter seclusion from the world and without a particle of food'. He was rescued but, sadly, died only three days later.

After such tragedies it is refreshing to know of someone who seems to have died happy. Such a person was Revd John Pinkerton who died in 1784. According to his memorial inside the church at **MARKINCH**, Kirkcaldy:

> *After having spent a very Chearful evening at Balfour House with Mr Bethune and his family he was found in the morning in his bedroom sitting in a Chair by the Fireplace with one stocking in his hand. Quite Dead.*

MASONS' MISTAKES

Mistakes were sometimes made by masons when cutting headstones. These add an extra curiosity value to a graveyard visit. Words can be inadvertently repeated, such as 'the the' on the stone of Charles MacKarter in **KILMUIR**, Isle of Skye. Non-existent dates occasionally appear, such as '31 April 1862' on the stone of Isabella Gilmour at **SANQUHAR**, Nithsdale.

Well-known places can be misspelt, such as 'Kilmarnockock' on the grave of Thomas Samson in **KILMARNOCK**, Kilmarnock & Loudoun. Basic spelling mistakes occur such as 'In Momery of' on the headstone of Sarah McLatchie at **CUMNOCK**, Cumnock & Doon Valley; and it was not unknown for a particularly proud mason to feel so humiliated by his own carelessness that he committed suicide. One such is said to have been the mason who, in 1722, misspelt 'Coldun' as 'Coldoch' on James Rankine the Younger of Coldun's stone at **KINROSS**, Perth & Kinross.

Another unusual sight is that of an unfinished epitaph on a headstone. An interesting example is found at **KILMUIR**, Isle of Skye, on the same stone that inadvertently repeated the word 'the'. The inscription reads:

> *Here lye the remains of Charles MacKarter whose fame as an honest man and remarkable piper will survive this generation for his manners were easy and regular as his music and the the melody of his fingers will ....*

But just what the melody of his fingers will do, we will never know. What we do know is that the mason was to be paid on completion of his work by Charles' son. But, when the latter was drowned crossing the Minch, the mason promptly departed.

STRANGE STONES

A graveyard is an unlikely place in which to find a modern-looking lighthouse and yet one is to be found at Kirkmaiden near **DRUMMORE**, Wigtown. This lighthouse, however, is only a few feet high and signals the grave of James Scott who died in 1852. It was erected by his father, Principal Lighthouse Keeper at the Mull of Galloway.

Another highly distinctive stone is to be found not far away at **WIGTOWN**, Wigtown District. It is in the shape of a stake and was erected on the site where Margaret Wilson, one of the Wigtown Martyrs, was drowned in 1685. Confusingly, it is now above the high water level, owing to the natural process of reclamation.

Perhaps the most idiosyncratic of memorials is to be seen at **TEMPLE**, Midlothian. The Revd James Goldie died in 1847 and his monument is inscribed with the details of his Will for all to see:

> *Bequest to the General Assembly's Education Scheme £100; to the Indian Mission £100; and the residue of his Estate amounting to £4000 sterling to the Royal Infirmary of Edinburgh under burden of a perpetual annuity of £5 to be given by the minister and kirk session to the poor of the parish of Temple on Christmas Day.*

EXTRAORDINARY PEOPLE

Some stones are notable for the physical characteristics of those they commemorate. The stone for James Weir, who died aged only 17 in 1821 and is buried at **CAMBUSNETHAN**, Motherwell, records that when he was only

13 months old, he 'measured 3 feet 4 inches in height, 39 inches round the body, $20^{1}/_{2}$ inches round the thigh, and weighed 5 stone. He was pronounced by the faculties of Edinburgh and Glasgow to be the most extraordinary child of his age upon record'.

Contrasting with this was the small stature of John Cowan. The following description of him has been added to his father's gravestone at WIGTOWN, Wigtown District:

> And his son John, of honest fame,
> Of stature small, and leg lame,
> Content he was with portion small,
> Keeped shop in Wigtown and that's all.

The KNIGHT *at* STOBO

Clearly John was the original small shop-keeper. However, any physical imperfections he had were nothing compared to a most peculiar looking character to be seen on a sixteenth century tombstone in STOBO Kirk, Tweeddale. We can only hope that the picture showing a grotesque cartoon-like figure of a knight uses a lot of artistic licence.

A number of adults are extraordinary for their age rather than their visage. At LEADHILLS, Clydesdale, John Taylor's stone states that he died 'at the remarkable age of 137 years'. At INVERLUSSA, on the Isle of Jura, Argyll & Bute, the stone of Mary MacCrain records that she died in 1856, aged 128, and that one of her ancestors, Gillouir MacCrain, spent 180 Christmases in his own house. How many he spent elsewhere is not recorded.

Such longevity is surprising, given the harsher living conditions in the past. Sceptics would no doubt suggest that people are as old as they feel and that they all felt older in those days. It may also be pertinent to note that all these cases pre-date the official records of Births and Deaths, which started in 1855.

For others the claim to fame is their name. One particular individual – Onesiphorus Tyndall-Bruce – takes some beating. He died in 1855 and there is a tower built in his memory on the Lomond Hills, Fife. His statue can be seen outside the church in FALKLAND, North East Fife. His remarkable Christian name is derived from the Greek and means 'a bearer of success or good news'. It was Latinised and became a surname from the first century. The name is found in the Bible in 2 Timothy 1:16.

An even stranger sounding name can be seen elsewhere in North East Fife on the wall of St Adrian's Church at ANSTRUTHER EASTER. This tongue-twister – Tetuanuireiaiteraiatea – is said to be the longest personal name on any gravestone in Europe. It is clearly not a local Fife name and indeed belonged to the adopted daughter of the Queen of Tahiti. It means 'the great God whose power extends to the heaven of heavens' and it does have a more exotic ring to it than the local Scottish 'Senga'.

The Princess was born in 1842 and at the age of 14 she married a Scottish trader, John Brander. They had nine children. He died in 1877 and the following year she married his manager in Tahiti, George Dairsie, who hailed from Anstruther. Thereafter she had a further three children. She must have married for love, because she forsook the tropical haven of Tahiti and returned with George Dairsie to the bracing shores of Fife when he retired in 1892. She became a popular local figure and, as her memorial stone shows, she died in 1898.

Another unexpected southern hemisphere link with Scotland can be found near the head of Loch na Keal, at GRULINE, Isle of Mull, where there is a large sign erected by the National Trust of Australia (New South Wales). It points to the mausoleum of Major General Lachlan Macquarie, affectionately known as the 'Father of Australia'. He was born on the nearby Isle of Ulva, but between 1809 and 1820 he was Governor General of New South Wales. During this period he encouraged the opening up of the eastern seaboard of Australia and, with the support of his wife, introduced a more civilised regime into the penal settlements.

Civilised behaviour was conspicuously absent amongst those engaged in the notorious Negro slave trade. They carried their human cargoes in appalling conditions across the Atlantic Ocean from West Africa to be sold as slaves in America and the West Indies. By the eighteenth century Britain was the leading country in the West African slave trade and legislation banning it was not passed until 1807. Some wealthy people took advantage of the slave trade to have African servants in Britain. One such person was a Mr M Murray, whose servant died on 3rd February 1776 and is buried in the graveyard on top of Trailtrow Hill near HODDOM,

Annandale & Eskdale. The gravestone shows the servant was ' … a native of Africa', who was given the name Charles Murray.

A couple with a less happy relationship than the Macquaries were a clockmaker and his wife from HODDOM, Annandale & Eskdale. His gravestone reads:

> *Here lyes a man, who all his mortal life*
> *Past mending clocks, but couldna mend his wyfe.*
> *The larum o' his bell was ne'er sae shrill*
> *As was her tongue, aye clacking like a mill.*
> *But now he's gane, oh whither? nane can tell,*
> *I hope beyond the sound o' Matty's bell.*

A contrasting description of a member of the fair sex can be seen on the gravestone of Jean Stuart in Greyfriars Churchyard, EDINBURGH. Her stone contains the lines:

> *A true saint I live it,*
> *So I die it, Tho men saw no*
> *My God did see it.*

The first three words contain an anagram of her name, with the letter 'i' standing for a 'j'.

The grave of someone else with an apparently unblemished record can be seen at WEST LINTON, Tweeddale:

> *Here Archbald Wilson's corps lies in the Grave*
> *Who in his life he did behave.*

To deter such people from becoming conceited, an epitaph at EASSIE, Angus, cautions:

Remember, man, that against death
There is not an antidote,
Be rich or poor, or what you may,
You'll die and be forgot.

Another gravestone also referring to the rich and poor can be seen in the graveyard by **ELGIN** Cathedral, Moray. The epitaph of John Geddes, a glover who died in 1697, adopts something of a philosophical tone:

This warld is a cite full of streets,
& death is the mercat that all men meets,
If lyfe were a thing that monie could by
The poor could not live & the rich would not die.

PUBLICITY *or* ANONYMITY

Publicising one's name is a favourite pastime of graffiti writers throughout history and in Orkney this was done in conjunction with grave-robbing. Since the robbery in question occurred nearly a thousand years ago, time has lent it a certain curiosity value. The chambered cairn at **MAESHOWE**, Orkney, is notable not only for being the largest burial mound in Britain, but also for its impressive  display of Viking graffiti, carved in runes, the ancient Norse script. The translations provide entertaining reading. We are told that 'these runes were incised by the best runester in the west, using the axe that Gauk Thaundilsson once owned in the south of Iceland' and that 'the pilgrims to Jerusalem broke into Orka- howe'. Clearly not all the Vikings were preoccupied by the pilgrimage while they were at Maeshowe. The runes inform us that 'many a woman, for all her airs and dignity, has had to stoop to get in here', and should there be any doubt as to what happened next: 'Thornj was bedded; Helga says so'.

In contrast, others chose to make their names as inconspicuous as possible. In 1603 the name MacGregor was proscribed – no one could legally bear it. The name was banned because of pressure from the MacGregors' powerful neighbour, the Duke of Montrose, with whom the MacGregors were feuding. Even Rob Roy MacGregor had to sign himself using his wife's name of Campbell. In the graveyard of the old kirk at ST FILLANS, Perth & Kinross, there is a gravestone which is supposedly to a Drummond, but on the back is carved a crown with a crossed pine tree and sword. These are the arms of the MacGregors.

The MacGregors' anonymity was forced upon them. Others were only too keen to have their names removed from the public gaze, as is evident from a gravestone at KIRKMICHAEL, Kyle & Carrick. The headstone of Gilbert McAdam records that he was 'shot in this parish by the Laird of Colzean and Ballochmil. For his adherence to the word of God and Scotland's Covenanted work of Reformation, 1685'.

In 1682, McAdam was arrested for his Covenanting activities. Following his trial at Dumfries, he was released on bail but soon re-arrested. This time he was transported to America to work as a slave on the plantations. He managed to buy his freedom and returned home. Whilst attending an illegal prayer meeting in a house, he was discovered by soldiers led by Sir Archibald Kennedy of Culzean (or Colzean) and John Reid of Ballochmyle. McAdam was shot dead while trying to escape.

When Presbyterianism was restored to Scotland in 1688, many found it politic to change their religious persuasion, including Culzean and Ballochmyle. Anxious to remove evidence of their past dark deeds, they had their names obliterated from McAdam's gravestone. However, 'facts are chiels that winna ding' and others were equally determined that they would not succeed in this. Later their names were re-cut into the stone by someone sympathetic to the Covenanters. That person was thought to be 'Old Mortality' himself (as Sir Walter Scott described the mason Robert Paterson), who devoted his life to restoring graves of Covenanters.

The second Earl of Fife also re-cut gravestones, not to hide his past, but to try to invent an illustrious one. He erected a mausoleum in the grounds of Duff House at BANFF, Banff & Buchan, but since the family's high social standing was relatively recent, he had no famous ancestors to claim descent from. Being a man of ambition, such a difficulty proved only a minor obstacle. He had an effigy and inscribed slab removed from Cullen Kirk, along with an effigy from St Mary's Kirk, Banff. He then proceeded to have new names and dates cut into them. The inscribed slab – showing a knight in armour and bearing the name Innes – was altered to show that it belonged to a Duff, who supposedly died in 1404. The effigy and incised grave-slab were returned to the Old Kirk at CULLEN, Moray, in the mid 1960s, but the effigy from St Mary's is still at the mausoleum.

Sometimes the removal of stones from graves can bring with it misfortune, as a footman to the Duchess of Bedford was to find to his cost. In Doune churchyard near AVIEMORE, Badenoch & Strathspey, the grave of Shaw Mor has five stones on it. Moving them brings down a fatal curse, as Robert Scroggie discovered when, in 1856, he removed them as a joke. Shortly after, he was drowned while bathing in the adjacent River Spey, and he too is buried in this churchyard.

Sadly, the five original stones were stolen in 1985 and have never been found. Maybe the perpetrator of this act of vandalism has since found to his/her cost that the ancient curse still works. As some consolation, five replacement stones have been placed on the grave, but they lack the distinctive shape of the originals.

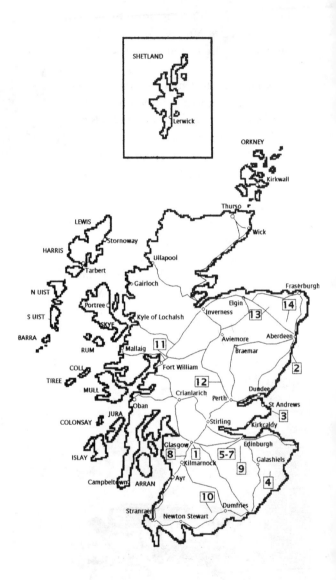

MAP 6 — RESURRECTION TIMES

RESURRECTION TIMES

Ref	Location	Description
1	Carmunnock	Orders of watch
2	Cowie	Watchers shatter gravestone
3	Crail	Morthouse
4	Eckford	Watch-house
5	Edinburgh	Mortsafe
6	Edinburgh	Watch-house
7	Edinburgh	Surgeons Square
8	Fenwick	Two watch-houses
9	Glencorse	Haunt of bodysnatchers
10	Glenkiln	Turner's Monument
11	Kilmonivaig	Gravestone with hole
12	Logierait	Mortsafes
13	Marnoch	Medical students and corpse
14	Udny	Morthouse

SURGEONS' SQUARE – EDINBURGH

RESURRECTION TIMES

For nearly one hundred years the ordinary citizens in much of Scotland were horrified and terrified by the activities of the Resurrection Men. Such men carried on a bizarre trade in a new kind of commodity – human corpses. This trade really started in the first half of the eighteenth century, but reached its peak in the period between 1800 and 1830. It has left a rich legacy of curiosities.

RAIDERS *of the* LOST ART

Trade in bodies arose because of the profits to be made. Demand was stimulated by the growing interest in medicine and the rapid expansion of medical schools. Scotland had a larger number of Universities than England but only one-sixth of the population and was renowned for its medical schools. As student numbers in Scotland increased, so more bodies were required for the anatomy classes. Bodies, however, were not easy to come by, being restricted by law to hanged murderers and the unclaimed bodies of paupers who died in the poorhouses. To supplement this supply, recently buried bodies were dug up and taken to the medical schools in centres such as Glasgow, Edinburgh and Aberdeen, either by students and their lecturers, or by professional gangs who negotiated the best price they could obtain.

Those engaged in such activities were known as 'Resurrection Men', 'Sack-em-up Men' or 'Body-snatchers'. Robert Louis Stevenson based his story *The Body-Snatcher* on the activities of the Resurrection Men and set it in the graveyard of the old kirk at GLENCORSE, Midlothian. This churchyard would have been an ideal target for body-snatchers since it was relatively accessible from Edinburgh but away from any village, surrounded by trees and out of sight of the road.

The Resurrectionists were viewed by the populace at large not only with disgust, but also with fear, since they worked furtively at night, frequented graveyards and exhumed corpses. The religious belief in the resurrection of the body meant there was a strong consensus view that people's chances of resurrection were not exactly enhanced if their bodies ended up in several pieces and in a variety of places. Sadly, few graves were safe from desecration.

BODY PROTECTORS

The main counter-measures were designed to render corpses less accessible by protecting them with physical barriers. Various methods were employed and their legacy remains to this day in a number of Scottish graveyards.

One approach was to avoid burial until such time as the body had lost its commercial value. This usually occurred after about six weeks. Small stone-built structures with strong locked doors and no windows, known as morthouses, were sometimes built to store the bodies for this period. The one at CRAIL, North East Fife, dates from 1826 and was built like a small castle. Above the door is the grim inscription, 'Erected for Securing the Dead'. At UDNY, Gordon, there is a round morthouse which contains a turntable upon which the coffins were stored. It was turned a notch every time a new body was placed on it, and once the coffin had completed a full circle the corpse was removed and buried.

A more common and cheaper alternative was to bury the body and then try to protect it by means of a mortsafe. This was a heavy iron coffin-shaped frame, weighing up to a ton, that was lowered over the coffin and retrieved for re-use at the appropriate time. There is a particularly impressive and solid example outside the parish church in Colinton, EDINBURGH. However, three much simpler mortsafes looking like cages can be seen at LOGIERAIT, Perth & Kinross. One of these is small and designed to fit over a child's coffin, since not even children were safe from the attentions of the Resurrection Men. Mortsafes were generally effective deterrents, but like morthouses were usually available only to the more wealthy.

A more extreme method of making a body less accessible was to bury it in a remote location. Johnnie Turner, a somewhat eccentric shepherd, had such a fear of body-snatchers that he excavated his own grave in solid rock

on top of a 1306 foot hill to the west of
GLENKILN Reservoir, Nithsdale. His monument stands prominently on the hilltop.

'watch out ...
RESURRECTIONISTS *about!*'

Friends and relatives sometimes kept watch
at night to guard a newly buried body. On
occasion professional watchers were employed,
but their reliability was often suspect. Whilst
the bereaved family paid them to keep the
Resurrection Men out, the latter often paid
the watchers to let them in! Those on guard
sheltered in small stone buildings constructed
near the graveyard entrance. These structures
date mostly from the period between 1820
and 1830 and their shapes vary from square
to octagonal to cylindrical.

A small attractive example of the last of
these, which is castellated and has its own
fireplace, can be seen at ECKFORD, Roxburgh.
A taller version with an upper storey occurs
at New Calton graveyard in EDINBURGH. At
FENWICK, Kilmarnock & Loudoun, there is
the unusual sight of two watch-houses in the
same churchyard. As there are two gates into
the churchyard, both had to be guarded.

Strict rules drawn up by the Kirk Sessions
governed the use of such watch-houses. The
1828 regulations are still displayed on a
board inside the watch-house of the church at
CARMUNNOCK, Glasgow. The watchers were
forbidden to get drunk, leave the churchyard,
admit anyone without the password, make a
noise, unnecessarily discharge guns, or do any

damage. Alcohol and gambling were usually banned, but since such regulations were unlikely to be enforced in the middle of the night they were usually ignored. Thus, during the long winter nights, the nightwatch often turned into a convivial drinking session which did little to improve the judgment or effectiveness of the watchers.

At COWIE near Stonehaven, Kincardine & Deeside, following one such revelry, the look-out roused his colleagues after spotting outside a suspicious black object that appeared to move and then stand still. Trembling from a combination of excitement, fear and alcohol, they opened fire. Gaining confidence, they ventured forth to investigate, only to discover that they had shot a gravestone, which had toppled over and broken.

Similarly at KILMONIVAIG, Lochaber, the local sexton, while keeping watch, shot at what he thought was a body-snatcher. The mysterious object was hit but did not fall. When morning came, the suspicious shape was seen to be nothing more sinister than a gravestone, but there was now a bullet hole through it as a reminder of the night's excitement. The stone still stands.

Occasionally the Resurrection Men were seen off not by guns but by ghosts. At MARNOCH, Banff & Buchan, medical students had raised and opened a coffin, but were forced to hide when they heard people approaching. Two local men were returning home and happened to glance into the churchyard. They were startled to see a body hanging half out of its coffin. After recovering from the initial shock and suspecting that medical students were responsible, one of them exchanged places with the corpse. Some time later, the medical students returned and nervously made their way back towards the coffin to retrieve the body. Their leader urged on his reticent colleagues, whispering, 'Hurry up lads and give me a hand'. No sooner was this said than they heard a groan emitted from the corpse and a croaking voice said, 'Leave me lads, I can rise myself'. This was too much for the students, who fled in wild panic.

whose BODY *is it anyway?*

The ghoulish trade in bodies reached its nadir with the activities of Burke and Hare. The latter owned a lodging house in a seedy area of Edinburgh near the Grassmarket. In 1827 one of Hare's lodgers died and he decided to sell the body. He enlisted help from another of his lodgers, William Burke, and they sold the body to the famous anatomist, Doctor Robert Knox.

Old Surgeons' Hall and the adjacent buildings in Surgeons' Square, EDINBURGH, were at the centre of the body-snatching trade in Scotland. Edinburgh was the largest of the Scottish medical centres and most of the leading anatomists, such as Dr Knox, had rooms in Surgeons' Square. It was here that the Resurrection Men came on their furtive nocturnal visits to trade their wares in return for cash.

Encouraged by such easy money, Burke and Hare became greedy and ruthless. To maintain a steady supply of bodies, and hence income, they resorted to murder, killing their lodgers or people enticed to the lodgings. In nine months they had killed between 16 and 30 people. All the bodies were bought by Dr Knox with no questions asked.

When their crimes came to light, Hare turned King's evidence and escaped penalty. Burke was hanged on 27th January 1829 and his body was publicly dissected. Dr Knox was not charged with any offence, but he was shunned by Edinburgh society and his career began to fall apart. He eventually moved to London and after his death in 1862 he was buried at Woking, Surrey.

As a result of such scandals and growing public disquiet, the 1832 Anatomy Act was passed. This licensed the anatomy schools, widened the legal sources of body supply, and introduced more effective sentences for grave-robbing. It brought the age of the Resurrectionists to an end and allowed the dead to be left in peace rather than pieces. Graveyards ceased to be scenes of frenetic nocturnal activity and clandestine forays by medical students and professional body-snatchers. Relatives of the deceased were spared the anxiety of long vigils on cold winter nights in the watch-houses. The poor ceased to be worth more dead than alive. The mortsafes became rusting mementos to the eerie era of the Resurrection Men.

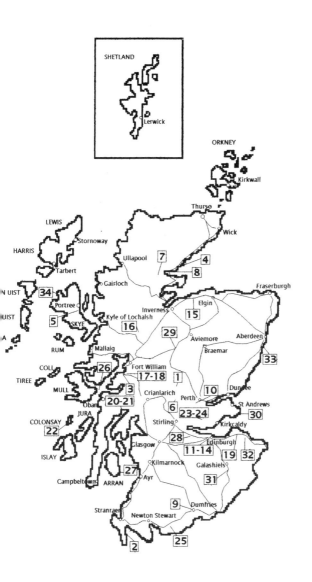

MAP 7 — JUSTICE, CRIME, PUNISHMENT

JUSTICE, CRIME, PUNISHMENT

Ref	Location	Description
1	Aberfeldy	Black Watch Memorial
2	Ardwell	Murder stone
3	Ballachulish	James Stewart's memorial
4	Ben Bhraggie	Duke of Sutherland's statue
5	Braes	Memorial cairn to Battle of Braes
6	Crieff	Iron stocks
7	Croick	Church with inscribed windows
8	Dornoch	Witch's stone
9	Dumfries	Mid Steeple Tolbooth
10	Dunning	Maggie Wall's memorial
11	Edinburgh	Canongate tolbooth
12	Edinburgh	Tolbooth Kirk
13	Edinburgh	Deacon Brodie's story
14	Edinburgh	Witch's memorial plaque
15	Forres	Witches' Stone
16	Glen Moriston	Memorial to Roderick Mackenzie
17	Glencoe	Memorial to Massacre
18	Glencoe	Henderson's Stone
19	Haddington	Iron hanging hook
20	Inveraray	Crank in Jail
21	Inveraray	Graffiti in cell
22	Isle of Colonsay	Hanging rock
23	Kinross	Tolbooth
24	Kinross	Jougs
25	Kirkcudbright	Jougs
26	Lady's Rock (Mull)	Site where wife was left to drown in sea
27	Lamlash	Monument to Clearances

Ref	Location	Description
28	Linlithgow	Plaque recalling murder of Regent Moray
29	Newtonmore	Gaelic notice about a legal victory
30	Pittenween	Plaque at site where tax gatherer robbed
31	Selkirk	Prisoners' Bush
32	Stenton	Tron
33	Stonehaven	Old Tolbooth
34	Trumpan	Trial stone

EDINBURGH'S PLACE *of* EXECUTION
– THE GRASSMARKET –

JUSTICE
CRIME AND
PUNISHMENT

Whether or not justice is necessarily dispensed by the law is debatable. It is not difficult to find instances where the system of justice has been used to enforce what seem to modern eyes blatant injustices. Few communities suffered at the hands of the prevailing judicial system as much as the people of the Highlands and Islands in the eighteenth and nineteenth centuries. For instance, following the defeat of the Jacobite rebellion in 1746, the culture, traditions, language and way of life of the Highlands and Islands were systematically assailed with the full support of the law.

It is hard to comprehend the so-called 'justice' that, throughout the Highlands and Islands during that period, allowed many thousands of people to be forcibly evicted from land their ancestors had worked for centuries and to have their homes burned down around them. This was done, often with great cruelty and inevitably with much distress, to make way for large scale sheep-farming which offered the landlords higher rents than could be afforded by their tenants engaged in subsistence agriculture.

It is therefore not surprising that such infamous events as the Highland Clearances have never been forgotten. The legacy of the

Clearances remains in the empty glens observed today in much of the Highlands, as well as in a number of moving and unusual memorials.

HIGHLAND CLEARANCES

Some of the most notorious and brutal clearances occurred on the estates of the Duke of Sutherland, in glens such as Strathnaver and Kildonan. The first Duke's presence still casts a shadow over the area – his statue stands conspicuously on top of a tall column on the hill of **BEN BHRAGGIE**, Sutherland. The monument was erected by his tenantry and friends, to his 'revered and cherished memory'. It is astonishing to find his tenants associated with this memorial, let alone bearing part of the cost, but in reality they had no choice but to contribute. It has not escaped comment that the statue's back is turned to the glens that his policies emptied and it looks towards the sea across which many of his tenants were forced to sail in a bid to seek a better life in the New World.

Amongst those who sailed to the New World were 86 people cleared from the Glen Sannox area on the Isle of Arran. In April 1829, they left Lamlash on the brig 'Caledonia' for Canada and settled in Megantic County to the south of Quebec, where they built a church that was identical to the one they had left behind on Arran. In the centre of **LAMLASH** there is a monument in the form of a rock erected by their descendants and dedicated to the memory of those forced to leave during the Clearances.

Probably the most poignant reminder of these sad times is to be seen at **CROICK** Church, Sutherland. In May 1845, following the issue of writs of eviction, the 92 people in Glencalvie were forced off the land to clear the way for a sheep farm. Most people sought shelter in improvised tents in Croick church-yard. Their sad plight is recorded in sorrowful messages, along with some of their names, scratched into the glass of the east window of the church: *'Glencalvie people was in the churchyard here May 24th 1845 ... Glencalvie is a wilderness below sheep ... Glencalvie people the wicked generation ... John Ross shepherd'*. This clearance was witnessed by a correspondent of *The Times*, who wrote:

> *Through the action of factors in the lonely glens, hundreds of peaceable and generally industrious peasants have been driven from their means of support to become wanderers and starving beggars – a brave and valuable population lost ....*

Not all communities stoically accepted the writ of eviction. Although the law was loaded against them, some hit back, as in the Braes area of Skye. When the laird, Lord MacDonald, tried to force the local people off their traditional grazing land, they responded by burning the eviction order and forcing the Sheriff's Officer into a humiliating retreat.

CROFTER'S HUT – SKYE

The response by the authorities was to dispatch 50 policemen from Glasgow to Skye. This provoked a hostile reaction: when five local men were arrested, the police were attacked and showered with boulders. The men were taken to Inverness, their fines were quickly paid by friends and they were released.

The resistance shown on Skye helped to draw attention to the wrongs suffered by the crofting community, with the backing of the law. The answer was to change the law and to remove the most blatant injustices. This was done in 1886 with the passing of the Crofters' Holdings (Scotland) Act. For the first time, crofters were given security of tenure, thereby preventing landlords from evicting them at will. The role of the local people in these events is commemorated by a cairn at **BRAES**, Isle of Skye. It reads: 'Near this cairn on the 19th April 1882 ended the Battle fought by the people of Braes on behalf of the crofters of Gaeldom'.

JUDICIAL MURDER

The injustices associated with the Clearances
pale into insignificance when compared to
judicially sanctioned mass murder. This, after
all, lay at the root of the infamous Massacre
of Glencoe. The Highland clans were seen as
a source of trouble to the king, William III,
as their support for the Jacobite cause meant
troops had to be deployed in the area instead
of joining the king's military campaigns in
Flanders. To remove this threat the Highland
chiefs were required to take an oath of loyalty
to King William III by 1st January 1692.
MacIain, Chief of the Glencoe MacDonalds,
missed the deadline. In fact he arrived at Fort
William in time, but was told that he had to
go to the Sheriff of Argyll in Inveraray. The
distance and bad weather meant the oath was
not taken until 6th January. This provided
the pretext for retribution.

A particularly chilling aspect of the
massacre was the use by the government of
mass murder as a matter of policy. The orders
came from the very top, being signed by the
king and sanctioned by Sir John Dalrymple,

The SCENE *of the* MASSACRE *at* GLENCOE

Secretary of State for Scotland. The orders stated: 'If MacKean of Glencoe and that tribe can be well separated from the rest, it will be a proper vindication of publick justice to extirpate that sept of thieves.' The Glencoe MacDonalds were seen as particularly trouble-some, at least by their politically powerful Campbell neighbours – the Earls of Breadal-bane and Argyll – whose lands suffered from periodic raids by the Glencoe men.

On 1st February, 120 soldiers from Argyll's regiment, under Robert Campbell of Glenlyon, marched into Glencoe. For twelve days they were entertained in the homes of the MacDonalds, after claiming there was no room for them in the barracks at Fort William and that they came without hostile intentions. This may have been true at that stage, but subsequent orders received by Campbell were to render such assurances worthless. These orders included the words: 'the soldiers will not trouble the government with prisoners.' And so, early in the morning of 13th February, the killings of Glencoe's men, women and children suddenly started. A total of 38 were murdered. The rest of the population of several hundred, escaped into a blizzard, though many of them perished from exposure to the cold winter night. A Celtic cross in **GLENCOE**, Lochaber, stands 'In memory of MacIan of Glencoe, who fell with his people in the massacre of Glencoe'.

The fact that even more people were not murdered suggests that not all the soldiers were enthusiastic about the role they were expected to play. Some retained their humanity and disobeyed orders. On the evening before the massacre, one soldier, whose hosts were brothers named Henderson, suggested they went for a walk. On reaching a prominent stone he began talking to it. This would certainly have captured his hosts' attention, if only because they must have wondered about his sanity. Roughly translated from the original Gaelic, what he said was: 'Great grey stone, you have been in the glen for countless years and witnessed many things, but if you knew what was to happen tonight you would not want to be here still in the morning.' He looked at the Hendersons and repeated the words. One of the brothers took the hint and did not stay in his house overnight. He lived to tell the tale. The other brother, presumably finding this all too ridiculous, ignored the veiled warning and paid with his life. The grey stone, known from this time on as Henderson's Stone (Clach MacEanruig in Gaelic), still stands in a field at Carnoch, GLENCOE, Lochaber, where it bears silent witness to this event.

The Lochaber area was later to witness another judicial murder, also involving the Campbells. This blatant legal injustice led to an innocent man being hanged for what became known as the Appin murder.

After the failure of the 1745 rebellion, the Appin lands of the Stewart clan were confiscated and Colin Campbell of Glenure was appointed as government factor. In May 1752, Campbell came to Appin to enforce further evictions, but before he could succeed he was shot dead and his assailant escaped.

Suspicion fell, possibly incorrectly, on Alan Breac Stewart. But, since he had fled, James Stewart was arrested instead. It seems he had done no more than make some uncomplimentary remarks about Campbell.

His trial in Inveraray, the seat of the Clan Campbell, was a farce. He was tried before a Campbell judge, by a Campbell-dominated jury. And, despite the lack of evidence, James Stewart was convicted. He was hanged on a hillock at BALLACHULISH, Lochaber, and this miscarriage of justice is recalled by a monument incorporating a stone from his cottage, inscribed: 'In memory of James Stewart of Acharn, who was executed on this spot on 8 November 1752 for a crime of which he was not guilty.' These events provided Robert Louis Stevenson with the basis for his book *Kidnapped*.

BROKEN PROMISES

Unjust treatment was also experienced by many Highlanders who joined the British Army. Between 1743 and 1804 there were 16 major outbreaks of discontent, including mutinies, by Highland regiments. They were a protest against what were seen as broken government promises, the lack of sensitivity to their distinctive background, traditions and culture, the harsh discipline and arrears of pay. Discontent was compounded by the fact that many Highlanders had not enlisted voluntarily into the army, but under pressure from the laird. According to John Matheson, for instance, who was recruited by the

Duchess of Sutherland: 'I entered not as a matter of choice but owing to the old feudal system of the country I was obliged to go to please the laird.'

Being misled about postings was a major source of bitterness. After the 1715 Jacobite rebellion, General Wade had formed six independent companies, recruited from within the Highlands, to keep order. They were different from any other part of the British Army in that they were promised that they would never have to serve outside the Highlands, being effectively a local police force to keep a watchful eye on their own area. They wore a dark tartan of black, blue and green, which contrasted with the red coats of the regular army. This led to their becoming known as the Black Watch.

In 1740 they were assembled at Aberfeldy and the independent companies were formed into an ordinary regiment – the 43rd. To commemorate this event, a memorial, with an imposing stone figure, was subsequently erected near this site at **ABERFELDY**, Perth & Kinross, in 1887. This statue is filled with tragic irony. It is modelled on an eighteenth century engraving of a member of the regiment. Unknown to the sculptor, the engraving was of Farquhar Shaw, one of three members of the regiment shot for mutiny in 1743.

It had not been made clear to the soldiers that, once part of an ordinary regiment, they could be posted anywhere and were no longer entitled to serve only in their own area. In 1743 they were sent to London and led to believe they were to be reviewed by the king. Their suspicions as to the real reason for being sent south started to grow and rumours were rife. At first they were to be posted to Flanders, then word spread it was the American plantations. Feeling betrayed, about 200 deserted to return home. They were pursued by dragoons and reached Northamptonshire before they were overtaken and rounded up. Three, including Farquhar Shaw, were shot at the Tower of London. The rest were sent to fever-ridden outposts in the West Indies.

Trouble about postings also broke out in Scotland. In 1778 the Canongate tolbooth in **EDINBURGH** was attacked by soldiers from the Seaforth Highlanders, following a mutiny by 500 men who thought they were to be sent to the East Indies. They were assured this was not to be the case and that when their overseas service was completed the regiment would be brought home to the Highlands and the men discharged. This promise, like many others, was broken. They were sent to India and discharged there in 1784 with no provision made for bringing them home.

In complete contrast, there is a welcome reminder near **NEWTONMORE**, Badenoch & Strathspey, of a case where formal legal procedures were applied in the Highlands to the benefit of the local people. In 1875 the path to the burial ground at St Bride's Church was blocked by the tenant of a nearby farm, with support from the laird. Local people raised a legal action to oppose this move. They won their case and the estate had to

provide a proper surfaced access route to the graveyard. To celebrate this victory, a public notice was erected at the site. The sign, written in Gaelic, can still be seen and reads: 'An Rathad Daingnichte Le Lach Gu Cladh Brighde.' Translated this reads: 'The Roadway established by Law to St Bride's Graveyard.'

ASSASSINATION *and* ROBBERY

At a number of places in Scotland there are reminders of past bloody deeds, including the first murder committed with a firearm. This was a politically motivated assassination carried out by James Hamilton when he shot James Stewart, Earl of Moray and Prince Regent. Hamilton, a staunch Roman Catholic, had fought for Mary, Queen of Scots against her Protestant half-brother, James Stewart, at the Battle of Langside in 1568. As a result, the Regent Moray had confiscated Hamilton's lands. Motivated by personal grievance and a wish to strike at those he considered were Protestant oppressors, Hamilton sought his revenge. His chance came when he discovered the likely date on which the Regent would be returning from Linlithgow to Edinburgh. With the help of Catholic sympathisers, he was given access to the Archbishop of St Andrews' town house, and a fast horse for his escape.

The house was ideally suited, being situated at one of the narrowest parts of the High Street in LINLITHGOW, West Lothian. On 23rd January 1570, Hamilton's chance came. As the Regent Moray and his entourage passed the house, Hamilton fired his gun and

The ASSASINATION *of* REGENT MORAY

Moray fell fatally wounded. Hamilton escaped to France. This murder is recalled by a plaque on the Sheriff Court House, which stands on the site of the Archbishop's house from where the shot was fired.

Another notorious event is also recalled by a plaque on a building – this time in **PITTEN-WEEM**, North East Fife. It marks the site where a tax gatherer was robbed, sparking off a series of events that culminated in the Porteous Riots in Edinburgh in 1736. The man responsible for all these dramas was a notorious, if unsuccessful, smuggler by the name of Andrew Wilson. He decided to recoup the financial losses he had incurred at the hands of the Excisemen by robbing one of their number. Wilson's chance came when he discovered the Kirkcaldy Collector was staying in Pittenweem. With his three cronies, Wilson attacked and robbed the Collector of the £200 which had been collected in duties. However, the Collector managed to escape and rouse the local militia. Wilson and his colleagues were soon tracked down and then arrested.

To save their necks, two of the gang turned King's evidence, leaving Wilson and his friend, Geordie Robertson, to face the gallows. Wilson, resourceful but incompetent as ever, managed to saw through a bar of their cell in Edinburgh's tolbooth. However, in trying to wriggle out of the narrow gap in the cell window he only succeeded in becoming stuck and had to be freed by his gaolers.

Wilson was not finished. On the Sunday before the hanging, the two prisoners were attending the Tolbooth Kirk in **EDINBURGH** when, at the end of the service, Wilson suddenly grabbed his two guards and flung himself at one of the men guarding Robertson. In the commotion Robertson seized his chance, broke free from his other guard and fled from the church. He was never recaptured.

Wilson's self-sacrifice made him a local hero. The authorities, fearing a rescue attempt would be mounted, summoned the City Guard under Captain Porteous to guard the scaffold. However, once Wilson had been executed, trouble broke out. In sheer panic, Porteous ordered his men to open fire. A number of bystanders were killed, others wounded. Porteous then found himself on a charge and, in turn, was condemned to death. Delays with his execution led to suspicions that he might be pardoned. To ensure this did not happen, the Tolbooth was stormed one night by a group of armed men and Captain Porteous was dragged away. The next morning his body was found swinging from a pole in the Grassmarket. Despite extensive enquiries by the authorities, no

A City Guard Captain *by* Kay

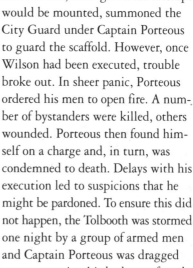

one was ever found guilty of partaking in this summary justice. It is curious to think that such momentous events stemmed from the actions of an unsuccessful smuggler.

CRIMES *of* PASSION

Murders are more often crimes of passion than cold, calculated killings and not infrequently involve jealous suitors of some fair lady. Such an event is recalled by a stone with the chilling word 'Murder' carved on it. It can be found behind the gatehouse to Ardwell House near **ARDWELL**, Wigtown.

In the sixteenth century, passions were aroused over the attractive daughter of the Laird of Portcorkerie. She was being courted by Messrs Gordon and MacDouall. When the former persuaded her to accompany him to the family residence at Cardoness Castle, MacDouall was distraught and later went to try to persuade her to return with him. This she refused to do, so the dejected MacDouall returned alone. Gordon, however, discovered what was going on and arranged for some of his retainers to get rid of his rival once and for all. The place where they caught and killed MacDouall is marked by the Murder Stone. Ironically it appears the lady then thought better of staying with Gordon and left him without the prize he had murdered for.

Marriage partners, as well as rival suitors, can be the intended victims of violence, as the wife of Lachlan MacLean was to discover in 1523. MacLean decided to obtain permanent separation from his wife by murdering her.

Since she came from a powerful family, being the daughter of the Duke of Argyll, Chief of Clan Campbell, MacLean had to ensure that no suspicious circumstances surrounded his wife's death. Eventually he hit upon the perfect scheme – or so he thought. One night he bound and gagged her in his castle at Duart, Isle of Mull, and rowed her out to a rocky islet in the Sound of Mull where he left her to drown by the incoming tide. In the morning, MacLean was relieved to see no sign of his wife on the islet, known ever since this episode as LADY'S ROCK. He lost no time sending word to the Campbells at Inveraray that their Chief's daughter had drowned in an unfortunate accident. MacLean, the distraught husband, earnestly sought to bring the body back to Inveraray for burial with her ancestors. Agreement to his proposal arrived by return.

A few days later the mourners, led by MacLean, arrived with the coffin at Inveraray Castle. They were welcomed in and invited to join the Chief for a meal after their tiring journey. On entering the dining hall MacLean must have come close to suffering apoplexy when he saw his wife, alive and well, sitting at the head of the table with her father. She had been rescued from the rocks by a passing boat, but neither this, nor how she had come to be on an islet in the Sound of Mull in the first place, was mentioned during the meal. No doubt MacLean's appetite deserted him. His hosts must have greatly enjoyed his obvious embarrassment and discomfort as he struggled to make polite conversation and to pretend that nothing had happened.

They even let him leave Inveraray unmolested, but MacLean must have known that his days were numbered. A few weeks later, on a trip to Edinburgh, MacLean was murdered in his sleep by John Campbell, one of his wife's brothers.

DECEPTIONS

The forces representing law and order can sometimes overstep the mark and turn to excessive violence, as witnessed, for instance, in the brutalities inflicted on Jacobite sympathisers after the Battle of Culloden. Many people were killed away from the battlefield when they were unarmed, although others continued to resist. One of the latter was Roderick Mackenzie, a fugitive after the battle when government troops were searching the Highlands for Prince Charles Edward Stewart (Bonnie Prince Charlie). Roderick, for better or worse, bore a close resemblance to the Prince and there was considerable excitement when he was discovered by soldiers. He chose to stand and fight but, hopelessly outnumbered, he was shot dead. With his last gasp he managed to whisper, 'You have shot your Prince'. The subsequent confusion over his identity gave the real Prince a valuable breathing space as the search for him was temporarily relaxed. The site of Roderick's death, beside the present day A887 near Ceannacroc in **GLEN MORISTON**, Inverness, is marked by a cairn telling the story.

Deception during his life rather than on his death was a speciality of the colourful

William Brodie, who frequented the High Street in **EDINBURGH**. His story is told on the side of the tavern which bears his name. 'By day,' we are told, 'William Brodie was pious, wealthy and a much respected citizen and in 1781 was elected Deacon Councillor of the city. But at night he was a gambler, a thief, dissipated and licentious. The annals record his cunning and audacity were unsurpassed.'

At first Brodie was successful in his nocturnal ventures, but when his activities came to light there was a public outcry and he was hanged from the city's new gallows on 1st October 1788. There was an element of poetic justice about this – Brodie had helped to design the gallows. His double character provided the inspiration for Robert Louis Stevenson's classic story, *Dr Jekyll and Mr Hyde.*

WITCH TRIALS

The supposed existence of a double character was the pretext for the cruel treatment handed out to so-called 'witches'. Witchcraft mania afflicted Scotland on several occasions – most notoriously in the 1590s, 1620s, 1640s and 1660s. Such times were often ones of religious fervour and the biblical text in Exodus 22:8 – 'Thou shall not suffer a witch to live' – provided the excuse for these persecutions. Harmless but eccentric, often elderly women were accused of being witches on the basis of wild rumours and scaremongering that played on local superstitions and ignorance. They were made to confess under torture and then killed by burning, drowning or strangling.

An unfortunate woman is commemorated at **DUNNING**, Perth & Kinross, where there is a curious stone cross with the words 'Maggie Wall burnt here as a witch, 1657'. The regular appearance of fresh flowers and new paint on the inscription show that Maggie Wall has not been forgotten locally.

The last judicial execution for witchcraft took place at **DORNOCH**, Sutherland, in 1722, on the peculiar justification that the 'witch', Janet Horn, had turned her daughter into a pony, which was then shod by the devil. This event is also recalled by a 'Witch's Stone' with the date 1722 carved on it.

At **FORRES**, Moray, witches used to be rolled down Cluny Hill in a barrel containing spikes and then burned. The site of one such burning is marked by the 'Witches' Stone'.

At the top end of the Royal Mile in **EDINBURGH** there is an unusual reminder of these persecutions. On a fountain, near where witches were burned at the stake, there is a plaque with a strange picture of two heads and a serpent. Their significance is not immediately apparent but, fortunately, there is an inscription to explain:

The wicked head and serene head signify that some used their exceptional knowledge for evil purposes while others were misunderstood and wished their kind nothing but good. The serpent has the dual significance of evil and of wisdom.

SUMMARY JUSTICE

The outcome of most witch trials was a foregone conclusion, but this was not the case with an unusual system of justice practised at one time in the churchyard at **TRUMPAN**, Isle of Skye. The part of judge and jury was taken by a stone pillar with a hole in it, called Clach Deuchainn or the Trial Stone. The system was attractively cheap and straightforward. The accused was blindfolded and then told to try to place a finger in the hole. Success proved innocence whereas failure indicated guilt. No doubt those acquitted trumpeted the virtues of Trumpan justice.

Another way of reducing legal formalities was to try accused persons on the spot and then immediately carry out the sentence before anyone could object. This can be viewed as Wild West type justice, although the west in this case was the Isle of **COLONSAY**. A rock called Am Binnean Crom (Crooked Pinnacle) provided an ideal gibbet and the natural hole through it was convenient for a rope. The rock is above the strand between Colonsay and Oronsay and is reputed to have last been used in 1615 to hang some MacDougalls. The story is that a MacDougall wanted to marry the Prior of Oronsay's daughter, but after receiving little encouragement he decided to kidnap her. He landed on Oronsay along with his three brothers, but was unaware that Sir James MacDonald and his entourage were staying on the island. The intending kidnappers were discovered, captured and hanged from this rock.

It was not just the west of Scotland that practised such summary justice. At HADDINGTON, East Lothian, in the seventeenth century, a fight over money scattered to the poor led to a fatal stabbing. The perpetrator was immediately tried and then hung from the iron hook still visible on the Nungate Bridge.

PRISONS *and* PRISONERS

Those formally tried and found guilty of custodial offences were imprisoned in the local tolbooth. But the cells in many tolbooths do not seem to have been very secure and escapes were not unusual. The motive in 1703 for building the present tolbooth at DUMFRIES, Nithsdale, was: 'the town is not at present provided with sufficient prisons, whereby several malefactors guilty of great crimes, and others for debt, have made their escape, to the dishonour and imminent peril of the burgh.'

At Selkirk, Ettrick & Lauderdale, the prisoners seem to have been less inclined to escape, at least on a permanent basis, because as late as 1833 they are reported as being 'frequently in the practice of coming out in the evening, and returning again before the jailer's visit in the morning'.

Selkirk's relaxed attitude towards prisoners was also very evident between 1811 and 1814 when 190 French officers, captured during the Napoleonic War, were quartered in the town. The Frenchmen were restricted to a one-mile radius around the town. The limit to the east of SELKIRK on the Bridgelands Road was

marked by a small thorn tree. It, or a successor, is still known as the Prisoners' Bush. Any prisoner found outwith the boundary was liable to a one guinea fine, which went to the informant. Such a reward was never claimed, even though prisoners frequently went fishing several miles down the River Tweed. There seems to have been a general consensus to ignore such infringements by the prisoners. For instance, Walter Scott, who lived some four miles away at Abbotsford, frequently invited prisoners over for a meal and to spend the evening with him.

Most prisoners had much more restricted opportunities to communicate with the world outside, although the Episcopalian minister of Muchalls, imprisoned in the tolbooth at STONEHAVEN, Kincardine & Deeside, during the mid eighteenth century religious troubles, continued to administer to his congregation through the barred window. People brought their children to him to be baptised – a scene portrayed in a noted picture by the Victorian artist George Washington Brownlow.

The opportunity to communicate with the outside world from inside a tolbooth was also noted in 1818 by prison reformer, Elizabeth Fry, at KINROSS, Perth & Kinross. The present tolbooth was described as having 'two miserable cells on the ground floor, one of which gave the occupant a chance to chat with passers-by on the street, while the other was a dungeon without light or air except through a grated hole in the door. There was no exercise yard. Prisoners were given four pence a day to keep themselves'.

Such miserable conditions were little better at first in purpose-built prisons. At the old jail in **INVERARAY**, Argyll & Bute, the eight small cells that once housed 29 men, women, children and lunatics can be visited. A crank of a different sort continues to be housed there. It is a punishment machine, the handle of which had to be cranked round by prisoners up to 14,000 times a day.

Despite these degradations, some prisoners retained a sense of humour. Graffiti written by Hugh Currie on the wall of his cell at Inveraray advertises: 'A room to leat to the 26 day of Jun. Aplication to be made to Doncan Campbell Jailer. Hugh Currie is out for Ever.'

NON-CUSTODIAL SENTENCES

The cost of enforcing prison sentences was high for most burghs, so there was a preference for non-custodial sentences. Amongst the less barbaric forms of punishment were fines, banishment or confinement in the stocks or jougs. The latter two methods relied heavily on public humiliation and ridicule. Jougs were iron collars that fitted around the miscreant's neck and were usually fixed by a chain to a prominent structure, such as the tolbooth or mercat cross. They can still be found in many towns and villages, with examples on the tolbooth at Kirkcudbright, Stewartry, and on the mercat cross at Kinross, Perth & Kinross.

Stocks, which confined people by the legs rather than neck, are much rarer relics in Scotland, although a set made of iron and capable of accommodating two people can still be seen at **CRIEFF**, Perth & Kinross.

STOCKS

Some punishments seem vicious by our standards. Trons, of which a restored example can be found at **STENTON**, East Lothian, sometimes had a set of jougs attached to them. However, on occasions the jougs were considered too tame. A more exciting (to by-standers, not victims) way of using a tron for inflicting punishment was to nail the offender's ear to the wooden post supporting the tron. It was even considered legitimate for the victims to reduce the time they suffered by pulling themselves free. This brought with it the painful disadvantage that the ear would be ripped. The local establishment also saw disadvantages in this course of action, but from a rather different perspective. Their concern was for the disruption to economic activity caused by the popularity of this bizarre form of spectator sport, since 'children played truant from school … weavers left their looms, and the women threw their spindles down' in order to get a good view.

JOUGS *at* DUDDINGSTON CHURCH, EDINBURGH

GEOGRAPHICAL INDEX

WESTERN & NORTHERN ISLES

Location	Map	Ref	Description	Directions
ORKNEY				
Burray	3	3	Block ships	In channel between Burray and mainland
Lambholm	4	27	Italian Chapel	E of A961 on Lambholm
Maeshowe	5	33	Viking graffiti	In chambered cairn 4.5 miles NE of Stromness on A965
Skara Brae	2	31	Stone Age houses	On W coast of mainland by B9056
SHETLAND				
Isle of Mousa	3	22	Broch	On W shore of island
Papa Stour	2	30	Maiden's Stack	At entrance to Housa Voe
WESTERN ISLES				
Castlebay (Barra)	3	4	Kisimul Castle	Offshore from Castlebay
Isle of Berneray	4	19	Parliamentary Church	NE part of island

NORTH HIGHLANDS

Location	Map	Ref	Description	Directions
CAITHNESS				
Mybster	4	32	Meeting House with spelling mistake	3 miles S of Mybster on A895
Reay	4	35	Jougs	On wall of church
INVERNESS				
Culloden	5	7	Battle graves	SE of Inverness beside B9006
Fort George	3	15	Impregnable fortress	On headland 7 miles W of Nairn
Glen Moriston	7	16	Memorial to Roderick Mackenzie	S side of A887 near Ceannacroc Lodge
ROSS & CROMARTY				
Cove	1	5	Cave used for modern worship	On shores of W side of Loch Ewe
Cromarty	4	7	Laird's Loft	East Kirk in Church Street
Tain	4	40	St Duthac's Chapel	Ruin in Chapel Road near sea
Torridon	4	44	Preaching site	Am Ploc at the head of Loch Torridon
SUTHERLAND				
Ben Bhraggie	7	4	Duke of Sutherland's statue	On hill above Golspie

Location	Map	Ref	Description	Directions
Croick	7	7	Church with inscribed windows	At end of road up Strath Carron
Dornoch	7	8	Witch's stone	In Carnaig Street
Golspie	4	17	Laird's loft	St Andrew's Church
Kinlochbervie	4	24	Parliamentary Church	In village

WEST & CENTRAL HIGHLANDS

ARGYLL & BUTE

Location	Map	Ref	Description	Directions
Carsaig (Mull)	1	3	Nun's Cave	At foot of Nun's Pass to SW of Carsaig
Crakaig (Mull)	1	6	Cave with remains of illicit still	On shore 1 mile WSW of Beinn Rendle
Davaar Island	1	7	Painting of Crucifixion in cave	S end of Davaar Island
Eilean nam Ban	4	12	Women's Island	Between the Isles of Mull and Iona
Ellary	1	10	St Columba's Cave	1 mile NE of Ellary
Fincharn	3	14	Wedding night blaze	Fincharn Castle at SW end of Loch Awe
Gribun (Mull)	2	21	Rock that crushed a house	E of B8035 near Clachandhu
Gruline (Mull)	5	20	Lachlan Macquarie's Mausoleum	1 mile SE of Killiechronan

Location	Map	Ref	Description	Directions
Inveraray	7	20	Crank in jail	In old Inveraray Jail
Inveraray	7	21	Graffiti in cell	In old Inveraray Jail
Inverlussa	5	25	Mary MacCrain's gravestone and longevity	In old burial ground
Isle of Colonsay	7	22	Hanging rock	Overlooking strand between Colonsay and Oronsay
Isle of Luing	4	20	Alex Campbell's warnings	On churchyard wall at Kilchattan
Isle of Ulva	4	21	Parliamentary Church	On NE coast of island
Killineuer	4	23	Skeletal handprint	By door inside old church 1.25 miles E of Ford
Lady's Rock	7	26	Site where wife left to drown in sea	In the sea, 1.5 miles ESE of Duart Castle
BADENOCH/STRATHSPEY				
Aviemore	5	2	Shaw Mor's gravestone	Churchyard near Doune – 2 miles S of Aviemore
Ben Alder	1	2	Cave (Cluny's Cage) used by Bonnie Prince Charlie	Southern slopes of Ben Alder
Newtonmore	7	29	Gaelic notice about a legal victory	W of town by bridge over R Calder
Ruthven	3	31	Barracks	SE of Kingussie on B970

Location	Map	Ref	Description	Directions
LOCHABER				
Ballachulish	7	3	James Stewart's memorial	At S end of Ballachulish Bridge
Glencoe	7	17	Memorial to massacre	Celtic cross on SE edge of village
Glencoe	7	18	Henderson's Stone	*On croft land between A82 and village
Glenelg	3	18	Barracks	At foot of Glenelg
Isle of Eigg	1	11	Cave where inhabitants of Eigg were suffocated	Cave of St Francis – at S end of island
Kilmonivaig	6	11	Gravestone with hole	In churchyard just to WNW of Spean Bridge
Kinlochmoidart	5	29	Coffin cairns	Near summit of A861 betw. Acharacle & Kinlochmoidart
PERTH & KINROSS				
Aberfeldy	7	1	Black Watch Memorial	By River Tay overlooking Wade's Bridge
Balhary	3	1	POW camp	SE of Balhary House to W of A927
Cleish	4	5	Sanctuary crosses	Around perimeter of churchyard
Cleish	5	5	Boundary stone of lair	W wall of churchyard
Comrie	2	7	Earthquake house	In Ross area across R Earn from village centre
Crieff	7	6	Iron stocks	Outside the old Town Hall

Location	Map	Ref	Description	Directions
Dull	4	8	Stone sanctuary Cross	Near church
Dunning	7	10	Maggie Wall's memorial	1 mile to W of village on B8062
Fortingall	5	19	Mound of the Dead	Across the road from the church
Glen Cailleach	4	16	Tigh nam Bodach (House of the Old Man)	Glen NW of Loch Lyon
Huntingtower	3	21	Maiden's Leap	Huntingtower Castle by A9 to W of Perth
Kinfauns	3	25	Rhineland castles	Towers on hills to W and E of Kinfauns Castle
Kinross	5	30	James Rankine's gravestone	In graveyard by Loch Leven
Kinross	7	23	Tolbooth	In High Street near junction with Burns Begg Street
Kinross	7	24	Jougs	On mercat cross in park off the south High Street
Lawers	2	25	Lady of Lawers House	On N shore of Loch Tay
Logierait	6	12	Mortsafes	In churchyard
Mawhill	5	35	Leckerstane	N side of B918 near road to Dalqueich
Methven	5	36	Graves of Mary Gray and Bessie Bell	N of Methven on the Dronach Haugh
St Fillans	5	37	Disguised MacGregor gravestone	In old graveyard by golf course
Tullibole	4	46	Outdoor communion table	In churchyard

140

Location	Map	Ref	Description	Directions
SKYE & LOCHALSH				
Braes	7	5	Memorial cairn to Battle of Braes	Above A883, 6 miles SE of Portree
Duntulm	3	7	Careless prisoner	Duntulm Castle
Dunvegan	3	9	War of One-eyed Woman	Dunvegan Castle
Dunvegan	3	10	Feasting to excess	Dunvegan Castle
Dunvegan	3	11	MacLeod's Table	Healaval Mor SW of Dunvegan
Dunvegan	3	12	Fairy Flag	Dunvegan Castle
Kilmuir	5	27	Mason's mistake on gravestone	Kilmuir graveyard
Kilmuir	5	28	Unfinished gravestone	Kilmuir graveyard
Trumpan	4	45	Church burned down in mass murder	Overlooking Ardmore Bay
Trumpan	7	34	Trial stone	Trumpan Churchyard
NORTH EAST				
BANFF & BUCHAN				
Banff	2	3	Duff House – legal wranglings	Just S of Banff

Location	Map	Ref	Description	Directions
Banff	5	3	Stolen and recut effigies	Mausoleum in grounds of Banff House
Cruden Bay	3	5	Original Castle Dracula	New Slains Castle N of Cruden Bay
Fraserburgh	3	16	Castle turned lighthouse	On Kinnaird Head
Fyvie	3	17	Figure of trumpeter	On turret of Fyvie Castle
Marnoch	6	13	Medical students and corpse	In churchyard
Slains	5	39	Smuggler's gravestone	In churchyard above Collieston
GORDON				
Kildrummy	3	23	Traitor's gold	Kildrummy Castle
Udny	6	14	Morthouse	In graveyard on W side of village green
KINCARDINE & DEESIDE				
Cowie	6	2	Watchers shattered gravestone	In churchyard
Dunnottar	3	6	Scottish Regalia hidden in 1652	Dunnottar Castle on clifftop
Kinneff	4	25	Church where Scottish Regalia hidden	Memorial in church
Stonehaven	7	33	Old Tolbooth	By the harbour

142

Location	Map	Ref	Description	Directions
MORAY				
Cullen	5	6	Gravestone with name changed from Innes to Duff	Cullen Old Kirk
Elgin	5	16	Gravestone of John Geddes	Elgin Cathedral graveyard
Forres	7	15	Witches' Stone	Outside Police Station in Victoria Road

EAST & CENTRAL SCOTLAND

Location	Map	Ref	Description	Directions
ANGUS				
Eassie	5	14	Gravestone 'die and be forgot'	In churchyard
Montrose	2	29	Water tower	Beside the A92 in the town
Saint Vigeans	4	37	Loch with water-horse	Under the church
DUNDEE				
Dundee	4	10	Head displayed on church tower	St Mary's Tower in the City Centre
DUNFERMLINE				
Culross	2	8	House of the Evil Eye	At top of Tanhouse Brae

Location	Map	Ref	Description	Directions
FALKIRK				
Airth	2	1	Giant Pineapple	At Dunmore Park
Blackness	3	2	Ship-shape castle	Blackness Castle – on the shore at Blackness
KIRKCALDY				
East Wemyss	1	8	Doo Cave	On the shore
East Wemyss	1	9	Pictish and Viking pictures in caves	On the shore
Markinch	5	34	Epitaph to Revd John Pinkerton	In Parish church
NORTH EAST FIFE				
Anstruther Easter	5	1	Gravestone with long name	S wall of St Adrian's Church
Anstruther Wester	2	2	Shell decorations on house	Buckie House
Crail	4	6	Arrow marks on church	St Mary's Church
Crail	6	3	Morthouse	In St Mary's Churchyard
Cupar	5	9	Covenanting gravestone	Graveyard by Parish Church
Elie	2	18	Lady's Tower	On cliffs to SE of village
Falkland	2	19	Marriage lintels	High Street and Horse Market
Falkland	2	20	Inscriptions praising the King	On houses opposite the Royal Palace

Location	Map	Ref	Description	Directions
Falkland	5	17	Statue to Onesiphorus Tyndall-Bruce	By the church
Lower Largo	2	27	Alexander Selkirk's house	Signposted from village centre
Pittenweem	1	14	St Fillan's Cave	In Cove Wynd
Pittenweem	7	30	Plaque – site where tax gatherer robbed	On house at E end of Marygate
St Andrews	3	32	Siege mine	St Andrews Castle
St Andrews	3	33	Bottle-shaped dungeon	St Andrews Castle
STIRLING				
Dunblane	4	9	Broken cross	On top of W gable of Cathedral
Killin	3	24	Beheading pit	Finlarig Castle
Stirling	3	35	Town walls	Back Walk
Stirling	3	36	Siege in 1304	Stirling Castle
Stirling	4	39	Divided church	Holy Rood Church

WEST OF SCOTLAND

Location	Map	Ref	Description	Directions
CLYDEBANK				
Faifley	3	13	Foundations of decoy city	Near right of way on moorland NE of Faifley

Location	Map	Ref	Description	Directions
CLYDESDALE				
Douglas	2	11	James Gavin's lintel	Memorial in a street N off the A70
Dunsyre	5	13	Covenanter's Stone	Inside church
Leadhills	5	32	John Taylor's gravestone	In cemetery in village
CUNNINGHAME				
Lamlash (Arran)	7	27	Monument to Clearances	In front of Hamilton Terrace
DUNBARTON				
Ardlui	4	1	Pulpit Rock	1.25 miles S of Ardlui on W side of A82
Helensburgh	2	22	Hill House	Upper Colquhoun Street
GLASGOW				
Carmunnock	6	1	Orders of watch	*In watch-house at Parish Church
HAMILTON				
Hamilton	4	18	Echo – Duke of Hamilton's Mausoleum	E of town in Strathclyde Country Park
Hamilton	5	21	Duke of Hamilton's Mausoleum	E of town in Strathclyde Country Park
Hamilton	5	22	Covenanting gravestone	In wall of graveyard of Old Parish Church

Location	Map	Ref	Description	Directions
KILMARNOCK & LOUDOUN				
Fenwick	5	18	James White's gravestone	In graveyard of Parish Church
Fenwick	6	8	Two watch-houses	In graveyard of Parish Church
Kilmarnock	5	26	Thomas Samson's gravestone	In the Laigh Churchyard
MOTHERWELL				
Cambusnethan	5	4	James Weir's gravestone	In graveyard on NE edge of Wishaw
RENFREW				
Bishopton	2	4	Misleading date on inscription	Formakin House

SOUTH EAST SCOTLAND

Location	Map	Ref	Description	Directions
BERWICKSHIRE				
Fogo	4	14	Laird's Loft	In church
Ladykirk	4	26	Church provided by James IV	In village
Polwarth	4	34	Refuge for Sir Patrick Hume	In church

Location	Map	Ref	Description	Directions
EAST LOTHIAN				
Bolton	2	6	House of La Belle Stewart	Lennoxlove House
Garvald	4	15	Jougs	On church
Haddington	7	19	Iron hanging hook	On Nungate Bridge
Stenton	7	32	Tron	In centre of village
Whitekirk	4	47	Church burned by suffragettes	In village
EDINBURGH				
Edinburgh	2	13	Cannonball House	In Castle Wynd North
Edinburgh	2	14	Carving of boy's head	Paisley Close in the High Street
Edinburgh	2	15	House lost at cards	Royal Bank of Scotland – St Andrews Square
Edinburgh	2	16	House won at golf	Golfers Land in Canongate
Edinburgh	2	17	Deserted dwellings	Mary King's Close below the City Chambers
Edinburgh	4	11	Letter 'S' sanctuary markers	In road outside Holyrood House
Edinburgh	5	15	Gravestone of Jean Stuart	Greyfriars Churchyard
Edinburgh	6	5	Mortsafe	Beside Colinton Parish Church
Edinburgh	6	6	Watchhouse	New Calton Graveyard

Location	Map	Ref	Description	Directions
Edinburgh	6	7	Surgeons Square	Off Infirmary Street
Edinburgh	7	11	Canongate tolbooth	In Canongate
Edinburgh	7	12	Tolbooth Kirk	In Castlehill
Edinburgh	7	13	Deacon Brodie's story	On side of Deacon Brodie's pub in Lawnmarket.
Edinburgh	7	14	Witches' memorial plaque	On E side of the Castle Esplanade
ETTRICK & LAUDERDALE				
Bowden	4	4	Laird's Loft	In church
Selkirk	7	31	Prisoners' Bush	1 mile E of town on Bridgelands Road
MIDLOTHIAN				
Glencorse	6	9	Haunt of bodysnatchers	Graveyard at Glencorse Old Kirk
Penicuik	3	30	Copy of King Arthur's Round Table	*On stable block at Penicuik House
Roslin	4	36	Apprentice Pillar	In Roslin Chapel
Temple	4	41	Inscription about Kirk Session controls	Temple Old Kirk graveyard
Temple	5	41	Will on gravestone	Graveyard at Temple Old Kirk
ROXBURGH				
Denholm	2	10	Text House	In village

Location	Map	Ref	Description	Directions
Eckford	6	4	Watchhouse	In churchyard
Kirk Yetholm	2	23	Gypsy palace	In village
Smailholm	3	34	Watchman's seat & lantern recess	Smailholm Tower 1 mile SW of village
TWEEDALE				
Linkumdoddie	2	26	House of Willie Wastle's wife	4 miles S of Broughton
Manor Valley	2	28	Black Dwarf's cottage	On E side of road up the Manor Valley
Stobo	5	40	Cartoon-like character	Inside Stobo Church
West Linton	5	42	Gravestone of Archibald Wilson	In churchyard
WEST LOTHIAN				
Bathgate	4	3	Cutty Stool	Bennie Museum in Bathgate
Blackness	2	5	House of the Binns	1 mile S of Blackness
Linlithgow	3	28	Vomitarium	Off Great Hall at Linlithgow Palace
Linlithgow	4	28	Scene of James IV's apparition	Inside St Michael's Church
Linlithgow	4	29	Royal coat of arms	In St Michael's Church
Linlithgow	4	30	Window with red lobster	In St Michael's Church
Linlithgow	4	31	Window showing childhood innocence	In St Michael's Church

Location	Map	Ref	Description	Directions
Linlithgow	7	28	Plaque on murder of Regent Moray	On Sheriff Court House
Torphichen	4	42	Sanctuary stone	In graveyard of Torphichen Parish Church
Torphichen	4	43	Disputed Laird's Loft	Torphichen Parish Church

SOUTH WEST SCOTLAND

ANNANDALE & ESKDALE

Location	Map	Ref	Description	Directions
Cummertrees	2	9	Unsuccessful holiday resort	3 miles W of Annan on B724
Eskdalemuir	4	13	Tibetan pagoda	Eskdalemuir beside B709
Hoddom	3	19	Beacon platform	Hoddom Castle to SW of Ecclefechan
Hoddom	3	20	Watchtower	On Trailtrow Hill S of Hoddom Castle
Hoddom	5	23	Gravestone of West African	In churchyard on Trailtrow Hill
Hoddom	5	24	Clockmaker's gravestone	Hoddom graveyard

CUMNOCK & DOON VALLEY

Location	Map	Ref	Description	Directions
Auchinleck	4	2	Misnumbering of Ten Commandments	Barony Church
Cumnock	5	8	Sarah McLatchie's gravestone	In the old graveyard

Location	Map	Ref	Description	Directions
Lugar	1	13	Cave used for coal gas experiments	On banks of Lugar Water
Sorn	4	38	Jougs	On church
KYLE & CARRICK				
Ballantrae	1	1	Cave used by cannibalistic family of Sawney Bean	Below Bennane Head
Dailly	5	10	John Brown's gravestone	In churchyard
Dunure	3	8	Spit-roasted cleric	Dunure Castle
Kirkmichael	5	31	Gilbert MacAdam's gravestone	In churchyard
Lendalfoot	3	27	Castle of 'false' Sir John	Carleton Castle
Maybole	3	29	Carved heads of gypsies	Maybole Castle
NITHSDALE				
Drumlanrig	2	12	Drumlanrig Castle	2.5 miles NW of Thornhill
Dumfries	5	12	Monument to cholera victims	St Michael's Churchyard
Dumfries	7	9	Mid Steeple Tolbooth	In the High Street
Glenkiln	6	10	Turner's Monument	On hill to W of Glenkiln Reservoir
New Abbey	4	33	Sweetheart Abbey	E end of village

Location	Map	Ref	Description	Directions
Sanquhar	5	38	Isabella Gilmour's gravestone	Parish Churchyard
STEWARTRY				
Kirkcudbright	2	24	House with Art Nouveau mosaic	High Street
Kirkcudbright	3	26	Laird's Lug	MacLellan's Castle
Kirkcudbright	7	25	Jougs	On Tolbooth
WIGTOWN				
Ardwell	7	2	Murder stone	*Behind lodge gate house of Ardwell House
Carsluith	1	4	Dirk Hatteraick's Cave	On the shore 2.5 miles SE of Carsluith
Drummore	5	11	Lighthouse gravestone	Kirkmaiden Churchyard
Isle of Whithorn	1	12	St Ninian's Cave	On shore 3 miles WSW of Isle of Whithorn
Isle of Whithorn	4	22	Church on site originally below high water	By harbour
Wigtown	5	43	Martyrs' gravestone	In the Parish Churchyard
Wigtown	5	44	Stone stake	Between the old railway line and the shore
Wigtown	5	45	John Cowan's gravestone	In the Parish Churchyard

*Denotes that the Curiosity is on private property or kept locked